The
JESUS
We Missed

OTHER BOOKS
BY PATRICK HENRY REARDON:

Christ in the Psalms

Christ in His Saints

The Trial of Job

Chronicles of History and Worship

Creation and the Patriarchal Histories

Wise Lives

The
JESUS
We Missed

THE SURPRISING TRUTH
ABOUT THE HUMANITY OF CHRIST

PATRICK HENRY REARDON

THOMAS NELSON
Since 1798

NASHVILLE   DALLAS   MEXICO CITY   RIO DE JANEIRO

Published in Nashville, Tennessee, by Thomas Nelson. Thomas Nelson is a registered trademark of Thomas Nelson, Inc.

Thomas Nelson, Inc., titles may be purchased in bulk for educational, business, fund-raising, or sales promotional use. For information, please e-mail SpecialMarkets@ThomasNelson.com.

Unless otherwise noted, Scripture quotations are the author's translation.

Scripture quotations marked NKJV are from THE NEW KING JAMES VERSION. © 1982 by Thomas Nelson, Inc. Used by permission. All rights reserved.

Library of Congress Cataloguing-in-Publication Data

Reardon, Patrick Henry, 1938–
  The Jesus we missed : the surprising truth about the humanity of Christ / Patrick Henry Reardon.
     p. cm.
  Includes bibliographical references and index.
  ISBN 978-1-59555-371-3
  1. Jesus Christ—Biography. I. Title.
  BT301.3.R42 2012
  232'.8—dc2   2011024313

Printed in the United States of America

12 13 14 15 16 QGF 6 5 4 3 2 1

MULIERI QUAM
ADIUTOREM MIHI SIMILEM
DEDIT DEUS

CONTENTS

FOREWORD

by Russell D. Moore

SEVERAL YEARS AGO, A BRUTAL STOMACH VIRUS CREPT through the seminary community where I serve as dean. One day, knowing that most of the students in my classroom were on the upswing from this sickness, I posed the question, "Did Jesus ever have a stomach virus?"

On a more typical day—a day in which the question of such illness would have been a more abstract reality—I doubt there would have been anything less than consensus. Of course, these future pastors would have asserted, Jesus assumed everything about human nature, except for sin.

But this wasn't an abstract question. These students were still reeling not just from the discomfort of the stomach flu but also from its indignity. They had been wracked with vomiting, diarrhea, fever, and chills. They still smarted from the sense of having no control over the most disgusting of bodily functions.

So when I asked this question, these ministers of the gospel hesitated. The stomach virus wasn't just awful; it was undignified. And thinking of Jesus in relation to the most foul and embarrassing aspects of bodily existence seemed to them to be just on the verge of disrespectful, if not blasphemous.

Why is it so hard for us to imagine Jesus vomiting?

The answer to this question has to do, first of all, with the one-dimensional picture of Jesus so many of us have been taught or have assumed. Many of us see Jesus either as the ghostly friend in the corner of our hearts, promising us heaven and guiding us through difficulty, or we see him simply in terms of his sovereignty and power, in terms of his distance from us. No matter how orthodox our doctrine, we all tend to think of Jesus as a strange and ghostly figure.

But the bridging of this distance is precisely at the heart of the scandal of the gospel itself. It just doesn't seem right to us to imagine Jesus feverish or vomiting or crying in a feeding trough or studying to learn his Hebrew. From the very beginning of the Christian era, those who sought to redefine the gospel argued that it doesn't seem right to think of Jesus as really flesh and bone, filled with blood and intestines and urine. It doesn't seem right to think of Jesus as growing in wisdom and knowledge, as Luke tells us he did. Somehow such things seem to us to detract from his deity, from his dignity.

But that's just the point.

The very beginning of the Christ story itself tells us that part of the sign of the Messiah is that he is wrapped in cloths (Luke 2:12). Why do you wrap cloths around a baby? For the same reason you might diaper your infant or wrap her up in a blanket. The point is to keep the baby warm and to keep him dry from waste. From the very beginning Jesus is one of us, sharing with us a human nervous system, a human digestive system, and as we'll see every aspect of human nature.

It didn't seem right to the world to imagine the only begotten of the Father twisting in pain on a crucifixion stake, screaming as he drowned in his own blood. This was humiliating, undignified. That's just the point. Jesus joined us in our humiliation, our indignity. In this Jesus is, the Scripture tells us, not ashamed to call us brothers (Hebrews 2:11).

The book you hold in your hand (or see on your screen, as the case may be) is the best treatment of the humanity of our Lord Jesus that I've ever encountered. Patrick Henry Reardon is one of the most Bible-saturated, Christ-intoxicated writers and preachers I've ever met, and I believe this is his finest work.

This book prompted me to think and to ponder. But, more than that, this book prompted me to pray and to worship, to see the Jesus it is so easy for me to forget: the Jesus who was really and truly one of us, so that we might be, with him, the heirs of the Father and the children of God. The one who took on every aspect of our flesh and blood in order to redeem us from the power of the devil (Hebrews 2:14–15).

As you read this book, I pray that you'll be driven toward the Jesus you might have missed. I pray also that you'll see something of what you've missed about your own humanity. Too often, we're tempted to excuse our own bitterness, our rage, our lust, our envy, our factiousness as "only human." The mystery of Christ shows us that such things aren't human at all, but satanic. We define humanity in light of our brother, in light of the alpha and omega point of humanity—Jesus of Nazareth.

This book will drive you to the Jesus you might have forgotten or might never have seen. It will also propel you with longing—for the day spike-scabbed hands wipe away your tears as you hear a northern Galilean accent introduce himself as your Lord, as your King, but also as your brother.

INTRODUCTION

THE ATTENTIVE READER OF THE FOUR GOSPELS MAY NOTICE
that they all contain—not too far into the story—a special scene in
which Jesus inaugurates his teaching ministry. Those first formal
sermons of Jesus—different in each of the Gospels—are preceded
by other accounts of his activity, particularly of his miracles. Each
inaugural sermon, moreover, introduces themes important to the
Evangelists. In addition, as the narrative sequence shifts from Jesus'
other activity to the beginning of his teaching ministry, the relevant
scene is introduced with a certain degree of solemnity, depending
on the style favored by the Evangelist.

In Mark's gospel, for instance, after three chapters describing
Jesus' other activities, the Evangelist slows the narrative pace in
order to introduce the first sermon in dramatic detail. Mark writes,

> And again he began to teach by the sea. And a great multitude
> was gathered to him, so that he climbed into a boat and sat on
> the sea; and the whole multitude was on the land facing the sea.
> Then he taught them many things by parables. (Mark 4:1–2)

Thus, the parables of the kingdom do not commence until the writer has determined the location, the crowd has been assembled, and Jesus has settled himself in the boat. Only then does Jesus begin to speak: "Behold, a sower went out to sow his seed."

In Matthew, Jesus preaches the first sermon, not at the lakeside, but on a mountain. Nonetheless, between these two very different sermons, the dramatic correspondence is perfect. After four chapters describing Jesus' other activities, Matthew suddenly adjusts the pace of the narrative to establish the *mis-en-scène* for the Sermon on the Mount:

Great multitudes followed him—from Galilee, and Decapolis, Jerusalem, Judea, and beyond the Jordan. And seeing the multitudes, he went up on a mountain, and when he was seated his disciples came to him. Then he opened his mouth and taught them. (Matthew 4:25–5:2)

Again, the writer determines the location, the crowd is assembled, and Jesus seats himself. Only then does he begin, "Blessed are the poor in spirit."

Although these are different sermons, each serves an identical function in its respective gospel. As the parables of the kingdom are programmatic for Mark, so is the Sermon on the Mount for Matthew. In addition, the similarity of scenic detail is striking: In each setting the crowd gathers around Jesus, who sits down—the posture of a rabbi—to teach them. Each Evangelist takes his time and deliberately adds details that solemnize the event.

In John's gospel the inaugural discourse, which follows two chapters describing Jesus' other activities, is developed differently from Mark and Matthew: The setting is private, the crowds being replaced by a single listener. The episode takes place at night, so we spontaneously picture a candle enlightening a small area in a shadowy room. In this scene Jesus' ministry as a teacher is established, not by the narrator but by Nicodemus, the only other person in the story: "Rabbi, we know that you are a teacher come from God; for no one can do these signs that you do unless God is with him" (John 3:2).

Then there follows the "God So Loved the World" discourse, which begins, "Amen, I say to you, unless man is born again, he cannot see the kingdom of God." This discourse serves in John's gospel the same sort of thematic role as the two sermons in Mark and Matthew.

THE SYNAGOGUE AT NAZARETH

In the gospel of Luke, finally, the setting of Jesus' inaugural sermon, placed after more than three chapters of earlier material, is even more detailed and elaborate than in the other gospels. Luke begins by informing us that Jesus had already been teaching:

> Then Jesus returned in the power of the Spirit to Galilee, and news of him went out through all the surrounding region. And he taught in their synagogues, being glorified by all. (Luke 4:14–15)

Luke does not relate the substance of that earlier teaching, however, so that he may portray the sermon at Nazareth as a true inauguration. This he accomplishes in stunning solemnity:

First, Jesus

> went into the synagogue on the Sabbath day, according to his custom, and stood up to read, and he was handed the scroll of the prophet Isaiah.

Next,

> when he had unrolled the scroll, he found the place where it
> was written: "The Spirit of the Lord is upon me, / Because he
> has anointed me / To preach the gospel to the poor; / He has
> sent me to heal the brokenhearted, / To proclaim liberty to the
> captives / And recovery of sight to the blind, / To set at liberty
> those who are oppressed; / To proclaim the acceptable year of
> the Lord."

Finally,

> He rolled up the scroll, and gave it back to the attendant and sat
> down. And the eyes of all who were in the synagogue were fixed
> on him. And he began to say to them, "Today this Scripture is
> fulfilled in your hearing." (Luke 4:16–21)

The people's response to Jesus further enhances the drama
of the scene. Those in attendance in the synagogue at Nazareth
that day thought they knew who he was: "Is this not Joseph's son?"
(Luke 4:22).

This was the same Jesus they had known since he was virtually an infant. Older citizens were familiar with his mother, who
grew up here. Some remembered that she was pregnant, years ago,
when she and her new husband, Joseph, went to Bethlehem (where
Joseph's family came from), to be registered for some Roman cen-
sus. Others recalled when they came back, the child with them, and
rumor had it they had spent some time in Egypt.

On that day, however, it was obvious to everybody that this was
not the same Jesus, or at least he seemed *very* different, when he read
and interpreted Isaiah to them on this Sabbath day. Something had
happened to him, so they inquired, "Is this not Joseph's son?"

The present book was inspired, in certain respects, by the bewilderment of the Nazarenes. In the pages that follow, I want to inquire: Who is this Jesus, what happened to him to make him appear so different to the citizens of Nazareth, and what other things came of it?

The scene in the Nazareth synagogue is a good place to introduce our inquiry into Jesus' life because it hints at two very different phases in it: First, there were the first thirty years of his life, when he was "in favor with God and men" (Luke 2:52). During that time he served as a boy apprentice to a craftsman father and later was a craftsman on his own. His was a quiet life then, at least in the sense that Holy Scripture says little about it.

Second, when we meet Jesus in this synagogue scene, certain dramatic events have recently altered the course of his life. It is clear that something profoundly transforming has happened to Jesus. From this point on, his is no longer a quiet life. He gathers disciples around him, and they all become so dreadfully busy "that they could not so much as eat bread" (Mark 3:20). What has occasioned this dramatic change in our Galilean craftsman? How is this change related to his prior life? What does it mean, and where does it lead?

The first four chapters of the present book will reflect on Jesus' life before the episode at Nazareth. The synagogue scene we will examine in detail in chapter 5. The later chapters will reflect on later aspects of Jesus' life, ending with his death and resurrection.

ACKNOWLEDGED DEBTS

Given the nature of its inquiry, the reader will observe that a proportionately larger part of this book is devoted to Jesus' formative years than is the case in the Gospels themselves. This is a fact, but let me qualify it with two considerations.

First, the "silent years" of Jesus' life were roughly thirty, whereas the years devoted to his public ministry—as we shall see—were probably just a bit over two. That is to say, the corresponding proportions in the present book are not really unwarranted by the actual division within Jesus' lifetime.

Second, in this book, the special attention given to Jesus' formative years rests on the author's persuasion that the foundations of a person's character are chiefly laid in his youth.

In this respect, I suppose, my presentation of the biblical material does reflect an interest that is admittedly modern. It is a quality of modern biographies that they tend to look for early influences in the lives they narrate. This has been true even of autobiographies for the past couple of centuries. For example, a full half of Rousseau's *Confessions* covers the first twenty-one years of his life.

Although the present book is in no sense a biography of Jesus (for the nature of the biblical material does not allow it), it is written from a modern perspective, by someone on whom the social and behavioral sciences have inevitably left their mark.

Even though this is a new book, I truly hope to say nothing new! At least, I hope to say nothing embarrassing to those generations of Christians from whom I have inherited the faith once delivered to the saints. If I pose certain "new" questions to the Sacred Text, I pray God they are not arrogant or pretentious questions. They may be, for all that, questions that Christians of earlier times, perhaps, did not think to ask. If this is the case, it behooves me to be, at least, devout and modest in the asking.

Nor is this a polemical work. At some points, it is true, certain recent theories will be challenged—especially in soteriology—but these challenges will be few.

Above all, this work will not present a revisionist Christology. I believe Jesus to be God's eternal Son, "of one being with the Father"—and all the other articles of the Creed. The reflections in this book are shaped under the beloved and gratefully acknowledged tutelage of the ancient councils of the Christian church. Those venerable authorities provide the interpretive lens through which the life of Jesus appears—in the expression of Gregory Palamas—as a *theandrikè politeía*, a "God-manly way of life."[1]

I confess a particular debt to the councils of Ephesus in 431 and Chalcedon in 451. In accordance with the first of these, I recognize in Jesus of Nazareth a "single subject"—one person, not two—who is God's eternal Son, of "one being (*homoousios*) with the Father." That is to say, in the scenes of the gospel we are not presented with two subjects, a "mixed" Jesus, as it were, part God and part man. He was (and is!) completely *both*. In the expression of Cyril of Alexandria, the most important thinker at Ephesus, Jesus is "a single reality" (*mia physis*).[2]

From the Council of Chalcedon I learn that this Jesus Christ is also "of one being (*homoousios*) with us." That is to say, the humanity of Jesus of Nazareth, as presented in the scenes of the gospel, is in no way diminished by his divine nature. He shares every single human trait as the rest of us, sin excepted. Nor, Chalcedon declared, are these two natures of Jesus confused, changed, divided, or separated. Both natures adhere to a single subject, described by Leo of Rome as "one person, divine and human" (*una persona, divina et humana*).

At the same time, I recognize that the purpose of those traditional dogmatic formulations was not to elucidate the Christian faith—for no light is brighter than the gospel itself—but to put a custodial hedge around it, a defining barrier to protect the Christian people from *misunderstanding* Jesus and the gospel. Otherwise, each generation of Christians—not to say every individual believer—might make of Jesus whatever folks thought best at the time.

Nonetheless, those who composed the dogmatic formulations of the Creed intended only to safeguard the truth of the gospel, not to replace it. It is the living gospel—the narrative!—that transmits the faith.

For this reason, my attention in this book is always directed to the divinely inspired writings of the apostles, that small collection of works we call the New Testament.

Unlike the later dogmatic formulas of the church councils, the apostolic writings tend—generally speaking—to speak of Jesus in narrative and existential terms; they are descriptive, most often, of the actual experience of believers when they gaze at the living Jesus.

Now, just what *do* we believers behold when we gaze at Jesus?

Well, let us limit ourselves to a single scene: We gaze at a man worn out from long hours of travel and labor, slumped asleep on the stern sheets of a fishing boat, which is being violently tossed all over the place by a fierce and dangerous storm. We behold this man's sailing companions, desperately struggling to keep the vessel afloat. They yell to the sleeper over the roar of the wind, to wake up, please, and do something about the situation. We see the sleeper wake up, glance around him, and then, addressing the wind and the waves, robustly tell them, in plain Aramaic, "Hey, knock it off!" The storm stops abruptly. Finally, the others in the boat look at one another and—understandably—inquire, "*Who* can this be?"

Fair question! *Who*, indeed? That is to say, even to those who knew him best and watched him do what he did, Jesus was a sustained source of mystification, and it is to our advantage that we ever bear in mind it is from *them*—those questioners—and *them alone* that we know anything at all about Jesus. Every single thing we know, we know on apostolic testimony. We must forswear any attempt to understand Jesus better than the apostles did.

This scene from Matthew 8:23–27—the story of Jesus asleep in the storm—also illustrates what I meant in saying that the dogmatic terms of the Creed were intended to *safeguard* the truth of the gospel, not to replace it. The Creed declares that Jesus was tired that day because he was human. The Creed asserts that Jesus was able to control the elements of nature that day because he was divine. Indeed, those who wrote the Creed were fond of expressing this double truth in ironic terms: God slept in the boat, and a man stilled the storm! The God and the man were the *same* person, a single subject.

IN THE FLESH

All true, of course, but those who wrote the Creed did not intend that its recitation should—or could—replace the experience of sailing in that boat with Jesus, receiving the multiplied loaves from the hands of his apostles, listening to his parables, beholding him transfigured on the mountain, washing his feet with our tears, and reaching out to touch the place of the nails. The purpose of this book is simply to help readers *return*, in lively faith, to

> *. . . those holy fields*
> *Over whose acres walk'd those blessed feet*
> *Which fourteen hundred years ago were nail'd*
> *For our advantage on the bitter cross.*[3]

This "return" is to the biblical narrative itself, as we read it in faith.[4]

Let me mention, in this respect, a foundational premise of the present book; namely, that the event of the Incarnation—the Word's enfleshing—was not static. To be a living human being, *any* human being, is not a stationary thing.

One of the most important Christian theologians of the fourth century expressed it best, I believe: The *being* of all created things is a *becoming*. Motion (*kinesis*) is a defining quality of everything God made. This is also true of human beings. Accordingly, the human race takes its rise and continues its course, not from a fixed "being" (*einai*), but from a dynamic "becoming" (*genesthai*). Human nature is not locked into a defining set of rigid conditions. On the contrary, it always bears within itself the "becoming" that marked its origin in Creation. Man has an essentially changeable nature; he is a stream, not a lake. His existence is a process, not a state.[5]

This process of humanization is what the Word assumed when he was made flesh and dwelt among us. The doctrine of the Incarnation does not imply an unchangeable human state—on the contrary, God's Son came to *change* it!—but a full human life. Irenaeus of Lyons, in the second century, gave voice to this truth about Jesus: *Gloria Dei est* vivens *homo*—"The glory of God is a *living* man."[6] The Word did not assume our humanity in abstract and philosophical terms. Rather, the Word became *a specific human being*, Jesus Christ, a man and the sole Mediator between God and man.

That is to say, God's eternal Word took unto himself not only certain human qualities but the concrete, historical circumstances of an individual human life. He made himself a subjective participant in human history, someone whose existence and experience were circumscribed by the limiting conditions of time and space and organic particularity.

An adequate Christology, then, should affirm that the Word's becoming flesh refers to more than the single instant of his becoming present in the Virgin's womb. He continued becoming flesh and dwelling among us, in the sense that his assumed body and soul developed and grew through the complex experiences of a particular human life, including the transition from preconscious to conscious.

During the entire period the epistle to the Hebrews calls "the days of his flesh," he continued to become flesh and dwell among us. In fact, we must go further and say that through the experience of his passion and death he "*learned* obedience by the things that he suffered." At every moment, even as he passed into the realm of the dead and rose again, he was becoming flesh and dwelling among us.

As a concrete human being, moreover, Jesus cannot be studied apart from the many human relationships that defined his history. Jesus was part of a specific society. He was a village Jew and saw reality through the eyes of a village Jew. His neighbors were the people at hand. He knew and loved them, and they him.

We have already reflected that we Christians have absolutely no historical access to Jesus except through specific human beings—his friends and followers—who wrote the New Testament.

They were part of a larger group who formed the actual world of Jesus of Nazareth. In the New Testament, Jesus does not appear like the garish sun, diminishing the other stars as it rises in the sky. Jesus is, rather, the sun that illumines those other stars and makes them visible. Several of these people—family, disciples, beneficiaries of his blessings—will also be found in the pages that follow. They pertained to the organic particularity of Jesus' concrete life.

Living a human life—we Christians are convinced—Jesus sanctified every human life in all its aspects, soothing every sorrow, redeeming all hopes. Perhaps no one has better expressed this truth than Gregory Nazianzen, called "the Theologian," who declared about Jesus, back in the fourth century:

Therefore now also, when he had finished these sayings he departed from Galilee and came into the coasts of Judea beyond Jordan; he dwells well in Galilee, in order that the people which sat in darkness may see great Light [Isaiah 9:2]. He removes to Judea in order that he may persuade people to rise up from the Letter and to follow the Spirit. He teaches, now on a mountain; now he discourses on a plain; now he passes over into a boat; now he rebukes the waves. And perhaps he goes to sleep, in order that he may bless sleep also; perhaps he is tired that he may sanctify weariness, as well; perhaps he weeps that he may make tears blessed. He removes from place to place, the One is not contained in any place; the timeless, the bodiless, the unbounded, the same Who was and is; Who was both above time, and came under time, and was invisible and is seen. He was in the beginning and was with God, and was God.[7]

1

GROWING UP

The earliest Christian believers knew nothing of Jesus' childhood because the earliest preaching—that of the apostles—had nothing to say about him prior to his baptism at about age thirty (Luke 3:21–23). This is the pattern reflected in the sermons in the Acts of the Apostles.[1]

Mark, writing the earliest of the four gospels, began his account of the Savior, not with Jesus' early years, but with the ministry of John the Baptist (Mark 1:2–4). Even the Evangelist John, whose first words take his readers right up to the eternity of the Word's relation to the Father (1:1–5), commenced his actual story by introducing the ministry of John the Baptist. Even before declaring that "the Word was made flesh and dwelt among us," this Evangelist proclaimed, "There was a man sent forth from God whose name was John." As far as history can discern, in short, the earliest apostolic witness contained not a single detail about Jesus' life prior to the Baptist's appearance at the Jordan.

In this respect, Matthew and Luke represent a dramatic difference because these two Evangelists have quite a bit to say about Jesus prior to the preaching of John the Baptist. This earlier material tells

1

of Jesus' miraculous conception, Zachariah and Elizabeth, Herod and the Magi, Jesus' circumcision, Mary's postpartum purification in the temple, the family's flight into Egypt, and their visit to Jerusalem when the Savior was twelve years old.

It is worth remarking that Matthew and Luke do not simply attach these earlier stories to the front of their gospels. On the contrary, each writer elaborates the material in ways consistent with the literary structure and theological interests of his gospel as a whole. Those interests explain why the perspectives in Matthew and Luke—notwithstanding what they have in common—are notably different.

Thus, Matthew's account of the pagan Magi, who arrive in the Holy Land in order to adore the newborn Jesus, serves to introduce a theological theme important to this author—world evangelism—on which, in fact, his gospel will end: "Go forth and make disciples of *all nations*" (Matthew 28:19, emphasis added).

Luke, on the other hand, uses the early stories of Jesus' life to set the stage for his pronounced "Jerusalem motif." These accounts enable Luke to portray three scenes that take place in the temple, even before Jesus' ministry begins (Luke 1:9; 2:27, 46). Moreover, Luke's account of Mary's song—the *Magnificat*—introduces some of the ideas programmatic of his gospel as a whole:

> He has put down the mighty from their thrones,
> And exalted the lowly.
> He has filled the hungry with good things,
> And the rich He has sent away empty. (Luke 1:52–53)

In these lines from Luke's first chapter, we discern various motifs he will later take up in the Beatitudes and Woes (Luke 6:20–26); the accounts of Zacchaeus (19:1–10) and the poor widow (21:1–4); and the parables of the good Samaritan (10:25–37), the rich fool (12:13–21), the wedding feast (14:7–14), the two sons (15:11–32), the crafty steward (16:1–13), the rich man and Lazarus (16:19–31), and the Pharisee and publican (18:9–14).

SOURCE?

There is an obvious problem attending these stories of Jesus' birth and other early events. The problem, which is historical, is easily stated: Just *where* did Matthew and Luke discover the historical material that fills the first two chapters of each of these gospels? Since this material had not been part of the early preaching of the apostles, *how* did the two Evangelists know about it?

The only reasonable answer, it seems to me, is that the "source" was Jesus' own mother, of whom we are told, "Mary kept all these things and pondered them in her heart" (Luke 2:19, 51). Later in the first century, when Matthew and Luke wrote, she alone was still alive to remember those details, which could have been known to no one else.

She was the living witness of the stories about herself and Joseph, the conception and birth of John the Baptist, the circumstances of Jesus' conception, the trip to Bethlehem, the manger in the stable, the swaddling clothes, the angels and the shepherds, the Magi and their gifts, Herod's reaction, Jesus' circumcision, the presentation in the temple, Simeon and Anna, and the dramatic event that occurred when Jesus was twelve. It was from Mary that Matthew and Luke knew these narratives.

What does this early material tell us about Jesus as he grew up? Taking Matthew and Luke as guides, I feel confident in the suggestion that the Savior's childhood and early experiences were chiefly shaped by two principal factors: his parents and his synagogue.

We are ready to look at these.

THE FATHER

Jesus' family bore Joseph's name. Although Matthew and Luke testified that Joseph was not Jesus' biological father, it was through him that both Evangelists traced Jesus' family lineage (Matthew 1:1–16; Luke 3:23–38). Jesus inherited the messianic title "Son of David," not from Mary but from the man who served him—literally—in *loco patris*.[2]

Jesus "was supposed" (*enomizeto*—Luke 3:23) to be "the son of Joseph," *Jeshua Bar Joseph* (John 1:45; 6:42). When he first addressed the citizens of Nazareth, those in the synagogue inquired, "Is this not Joseph's son?" (Luke 4:22).

Matthew provides an instructive variation on this question: "Is this not *the craftsman's* son?" (Matthew 13:55). The underlying Greek noun here, usually translated as "carpenter," is *tekton*, a term including any sort of builder, craftsman, or skilled worker—even a blacksmith. A *tekton* was someone who constructed and fashioned things with his hands.

In short, Joseph taught Jesus those cultivated manual talents summarized by George Eliot as the inheritance bequeathed from a craftsman father: "the mechanical instinct, the keen sensibility to harmony, the unconscious skill of the modeling hand."

Joseph passed these technical skills on to Jesus, who was also known as a *tekton*. A *tekton* was a man with talented hands, and Jesus' hands could heal the sick and injured! Mark surely recognized the irony of calling Jesus a *tekton* in the context of his miracles and teaching: "And what wisdom is this which is given to him, that such mighty works are performed *by his hands*. Is this not the *tekton?*" (Mark 6:2–3, emphasis added).

What more did Jesus learn from Joseph? Let me suggest that he also found in Joseph an ideal son of Abraham—that is to say, a man who lived, as Abraham did, *by faith*.

Consider the calling of Joseph. Every vocation is unique—in the sense that the Good Shepherd calls each of his sheep by its own proper name—but there was something supremely unique in the vocation of Joseph, who was called to be the foster father of God's Son and the protector of that divine Son's virgin mother. Joseph's vocation was not only difficult; it was impossible! In a sense, Joseph had to figure it out as he went along, simply following God's call, as best he could, wherever it led. He was obliged to leave the heavy lifting to God.

With so distinctive and demanding a vocation, Joseph might be excused, if, on occasion—the flight into Egypt, for instance—he felt anxious and insecure. The evidence, however, indicates that this was not the case. Joseph was not a person given to anxiety. He appeared, rather, as a man of extraordinary serenity. We find Joseph in five scenes in the gospel of Matthew, and every single time he is sound asleep (Matthew 1:20–24; 2:12, 13, 19, 22). Whatever troubles Joseph endured, they did not include insomnia.

Perhaps we see Joseph's mark on Jesus—particularly the example of his serenity and simple trust in God—when we contemplate a later New Testament scene:

> Now when they had left the multitude, they took Jesus along in
> the boat as he was. And other little boats were also with him.
> And a great windstorm arose, and the waves beat into the boat,
> so that it was already filling. But he was in the stern, asleep on a
> pillow. (Mark 4:36–38)

THE MOTHER

Most of what we know of Jesus' mother comes from the gospel of Luke, where we learn of God's message to her, conveyed by the angel Gabriel, inviting her to become the virgin mother of his Son. In

Luke we learn, too, of her acceptance of God's plan for her life, the miraculous conception of that Son through the power of the Holy Spirit, Mary's visit to Elizabeth, her meeting with the old couple in the temple, and the later incident when Jesus was lost in Jerusalem for three days.

In all these stories, the most significant fact about Mary was her consent to God's invitation. Absolutely everything else recorded in the four gospels depended on that consent.

Mary's "Be it done unto me according to your word" (Luke 1:38) was also the first step along the road to Jesus' "Not my will, but Yours, be done" (22:42).

I believe the correspondence between these two verses indicates, likewise, the important spiritual mark of Mary on her son. It was from her that he learned to respond in faith to the call of God, not counting the cost. Their destinies were inextricably entwined in the mystery of redemption.

Even as Simeon prophesied that Jesus was "destined for the fall and rising of many in Israel, and for a sign of contradiction," the old man took care to warn Mary, "Yes, a sword will pierce through your own soul also" (Luke 2:34–35). This prophecy was mainly fulfilled on Mount Calvary, where "there stood by the cross of Jesus his mother" (John 19:25), loyally adhering to him unto the end. For this reason we find Mary—in the New Testament's last mention of her—gathered with the other Christians in the Upper Room, awaiting the coming of the Holy Spirit (Acts 1:14).

The message Mary received through Gabriel foretold mysterious things about the coming child:

> He will be great, and will be called the Son of the Highest; and
> the Lord God will give him the throne of his father David. And
> he will reign over the house of Jacob forever, and of his kingdom
> there will be no end. (Luke 1:32–33)

It is beyond doubt that Mary understood she was becoming the mother of the Messiah, because such was the message these words conveyed. Yet, what did it all mean in practice? Where would it all lead?

Mary surely derived a further sense of her son's destiny when, at her greeting, the unborn infant in Elizabeth's womb suddenly "leaped for joy" (1:44). Then, at Jesus' birth, more angels appeared, this time to tell the shepherds,

> Do not be afraid, for behold, I bring you good tidings of great joy which will be to all people. For there is born to you this day in the city of David a Savior, who is the Lord Messiah. (Luke 2:10–11)

What did all this portend, and what further was the Messiah's mother to do? There is nothing in the Sacred Text to suggest the Messiah's mother understood these things very clearly. (Do *we*?) All we know for certain is that "Mary kept all these things and pondered them in her heart" (Luke 2:19).

For the rest, she walked in faith and thereby taught her son to walk in faith. Gradually, day by day, "the child grew and became strong, filled with wisdom; and the grace of God was upon him" (Luke 2:40), but not much happened that was extraordinary.

Indeed, Jesus seemed so ordinary a child that Mary and Joseph were quite stunned when, at age twelve, he suddenly asked them, "Did you not know that I must be about the things of my Father?" (2:49). Even then, however, Jesus "went down with them and came to Nazareth, and was subject to them" (2:51). That is to say, things promptly returned to normal.

Year followed year, and Jesus remained at home with Joseph, eventually taking over the workshop when Joseph passed away. Nothing out of the ordinary happened, as far as we know. If Jesus really *was* the Messiah, there was no outward sign of it. We may imagine Mary was content, living in company with her son, who was dutiful and conscientious. It is difficult to imagine she was unaware of his piety and love of study, but Holy Scripture does not comment on it.

Then one day, Jesus announced that he was going to see his cousin John, who was preaching and baptizing in the Jordan Valley. He left his mother at home in Nazareth, and when he returned some time later, everything had changed.

THE SYNAGOGUE

Everyone who knew him was aware that Jesus had no formal training as a rabbi. He was a workman. Unlike Saul of Tarsus, Jesus had not been privileged to study "at the feet of Gamaliel" (Acts 22:3) or some other leading rabbinic scholar of the time. Indeed, when the Savior—at about age thirty (Luke 3:23)—commenced teaching in the Galilean synagogues (4:15), his neighbors expressed no little consternation about it: "How does this man know letters, never having studied?" (John 7:15).

It would be wrong, on the other hand, to ascribe an absolute sense to their low assessment of Jesus' education or fail to consider its context. That is to say, the wonderment of Jesus' contemporaries was prompted by his ability to hold his own in debate with—and even prevail over—the recognized rabbinical experts of his day. His townsfolk did *not* mean Jesus was unfamiliar with Sacred Letters.

There is no doubt that Jesus was literate, for we find him reading, and there is every reason to believe he learned the Scriptures as did any other young man from a working-class Galilean family: at the local synagogue. Normally, in fact, in a small town such as Nazareth, copies of the Scriptures, or any other books, were available only at the synagogue.

Now, Luke testifies that Jesus attended normal assemblies at the synagogue each Sabbath, "according to his custom" (Luke 4:16). As it happens, we know a thing or two about this "custom" (*eiothos*) of weekly synagogue attendance, and what we know precludes any fancy that it was a thing taken lightly—a perfunctory minimum observance.

On the contrary, regular attendance at the local synagogue required a very substantial commitment of effort and time: first, it occupied most of the Sabbath. Flavius Josephus, a Jewish historian contemporary with the New Testament, spelled out the details for his Roman audience:

> We spend every seventh day in the study of the customs (*ethon*) and Law, regarding concern for these things to be important— like everything else—so that we may avoid sin.[3]

In short, everyone familiar with the Judaism of the day was aware that "Moses had throughout many generations those who preached him in every city, being read in the synagogues every Sabbath" (Acts 15:21). Besides the Sabbath, the two weekly fast days—Monday and Thursday (*Didache* 8.1; Luke 18:12)—were also occasions for public Scripture readings in the synagogue.

In the synagogues of Palestine, these public readings, following a common lectionary based on the calendar of Jewish festal seasons, were measured out so that the entire Pentateuch was completed every three and a half years. To these were added selections from the rest of the Hebrew Scriptures. Eventually some of this material was determined by particular feast days: Esther at Purim, the Song of Solomon at Passover, Ecclesiastes at Sukkoth, Ruth at Pentecost, and so on. We are uncertain, however, if—or how much—these patterns were fixed in Jesus' time.

After the public reading in Hebrew, the Scriptures were repeated in translations in the common spoken language—Aramaic in Palestine, mainly Greek elsewhere—so that God's Word would be understood by the people. Since our first example for this practice of a public reading in translation comes from the early postexilic period (Nehemiah 8:1–8), it appears that the pattern commenced during the mid-sixth century BC—the Babylonian Captivity—when the local synagogue became the defining and essential social institution in Jewish life.

Nor was biblical study in the synagogue restricted to public readings on three days during the week. The *Mishnah* testifies that the Scriptures were constantly maintained in the synagogue—under supervision—so that at any time a literate person with sufficient leisure might come and study them. According to Jerusalem's *Ophel Inscription* (contemporary with the New Testament), the synagogue was to provide adequate facilities to "read the Torah and teach the commandments."

For this reason, the synagogue was called the *beth hasepher,* the "house of the book." It was chiefly a place of study, where primary attention was given to the Torah and the other Sacred Writings. That is to say, the culture of the synagogue was literary; it was text based, a pursuit of the *ketubim,* the sacred *grammata* identified as God's Word.

Indeed, often enough it was at the synagogue—in special rooms or a courtyard or an attached building—that a young Jew learned the art of reading. It seems likely that Jesus learned to read in that setting.

When Luke tells of Jesus' return to Nazareth, he describes the town as the place where Jesus—according to the New King James Version—"had been brought up" (Luke 4:16). The Greek expression here is *tethrammenos,* literally "had been nourished," an expression referring to Jesus' nurture as a child. Inasmuch as "Jesus increased in wisdom *and* stature," however, this early nourishment should be understood as both physical and spiritual. That is to say, in returning to the synagogue at Nazareth, Jesus was coming back to the place where his soul had been fed during all those years of his youth. Moreover, the institution of the synagogue remained important to him throughout his life.[4]

In our own age, when most Bible reading is done at home and privately, it seems important to stress the social setting of Jesus' study of Holy Scripture. The synagogue context, a setting inherited from Israel's history, provided the atmosphere in which the youthful Jesus, reading the Sacred Scrolls, took possession of his own identity as a child of Abraham and a partaker of the Mosaic covenant.

Consequently, we need to consider more carefully what these Sacred Writings meant to Jesus as he matured. They were an indispensable element of his experience *in the flesh*.

JESUS AND THE SCRIPTURES

Someone who embarks on writing a biography—especially of a statesman, a religious leader, a philosopher, or a literary figure—should be prepared to cite the "influences" brought to bear on the conscience and thinking of his subject. We commonly expect this in a biographical account.

Thus, for instance, if I were to write a life story of Russell Kirk, I should devote some consideration to his early and very serious study of the Stoic, Marcus Aurelius. The calm and clarity of Kirk's thought—by his own admission—owed a great deal to his careful examination of ancient Stoicism.

We must admit, however, that such an approach to biography does not work quite so well for understanding Jesus! Although he certainly read Isaiah and Daniel, it is legitimate to doubt that the Savior of the world read Isaiah and Daniel the way Macaulay and Acton read Johnson and Burke. I, for one, find it difficult to picture adolescent Jesus looking up suddenly one day from a page of Job or Chronicles and exclaiming, "Wow, what an insight! That really does make sense!"

Jesus was not "working out" a religious theory. He was taking possession of his own identity. This was a process of growth, and Jesus' study of the Hebrew Scriptures was integral to that growth. He *did* read books, and he *learned* from them. The works of Moses, David, Jeremiah, and the others truly contoured his mind and conscience. The mental horizon of Jesus, as we discern it in the four gospels, took shape during those long years at Nazareth, where— Luke tells us—he went to the synagogue "according to his custom."

So when Luke also tells us, "Jesus increased in wisdom and stature," it is wrong to imagine his growth was unrelated to what he read—any more than his increase in stature was unrelated to what he ate (Luke 2:52).

Luke is our chief source on this matter. In fact, he is the Evangelist who describes Jesus reading and interpreting Isaiah near the very beginning of his public ministry (Luke 4:16–21). In the thirteenth century, when Bonaventure of Fidanza crafted his long and detailed commentary on the gospel of Luke, he prefaced that work by a discourse on the scene of Jesus reading Isaiah in the synagogue at Nazareth. For Bonaventure, this story of Jesus reading in the synagogue was the true key to understanding the Gospel According to Luke.

Bonaventure's approach showed great insight into Luke's intention, I believe; the correct understanding of Jesus—the task of Christian theology—is rooted in Jesus' *self*-understanding, and Jesus' self-understanding was inseparable from his reading of the Hebrew Scriptures.

Nonetheless, to speak of the "influence" of the Hebrew Scriptures on Jesus's mind dramatically transcends our normal use of that expression. The Law and the Prophets shaped his self-awareness in an unparalleled way because the Savior found in those writings his identity, vocation, and mission. His grasp of those texts—an understanding at the root of Christian theology—is the very substance of Jesus' "self-regard." It was in studying the Hebrew Bible that Jesus became convinced, "I must be about the things of my Father" (Luke 2:49).

What David and Isaiah wrote, then, was not something different from who Jesus knew himself to be and what his Father summoned him to do. Later on, in the very act of sending the apostles out to evangelize the world, Jesus "opened their understanding, that they might comprehend the Scriptures" (Luke 24:45). The proclamation of the gospel was to include the incorporation of the Hebrew Scriptures. Christian theology begins with—and is inseparable from—understanding the Old Testament as Jesus understood it. I will return to this consideration later, when we examine the Savior's revelation to the two disciples on the road to Emmaus.

The gospel of Luke indicates, moreover, that this understanding *increased* in Jesus. It did not happen all at once, because human understanding always takes time. Jesus *took personal possession* of the Hebrew Bible as he lived and ministered, as he suffered, died, and rose again. As events unfolded in his life—and particularly when he "endured such contradiction of sinners against himself" (Hebrews 12:3)—Jesus grasped ever more explicitly the meaning of God's Word. These books governed his life and destiny.

THE SON'S SELF

Thus, when Jesus read of Isaac's burden in Genesis, the paschal lamb in Exodus, the sin offering in Leviticus, David's opprobrium in Samuel, the "pierced side" in Zechariah, the Suffering Servant in Isaiah, and the persecuted just man in the book of Psalms, he found himself, text by text, to be in all of them. They were components of who he knew he was. Already, at age twelve, he had begun to grasp that these themes had to do with "the things of my Father" (Luke 2:49).

I believe it is misleading, however, to inquire "when" with respect to Jesus' self-knowledge. Self-knowledge is not objective. One does not acquire it as "information," like the study of biology or business law.

Self-knowledge is an extension and activity of the self; it is, by definition, subjective. It is necessarily tautological—that is to say, self-knowledge is its own cause. The knowledge of one's self is inseparable from *being* oneself.[5]

It is important not to "objectify" Jesus' self-awareness and then try to determine at what point—"when?"—he acquired the knowledge of his identity. Self-knowledge is intrinsic to, and an extension of, self-being. His consciousness of his identity *came from* his identity.

Self-knowledge, however, does take place in a process of growth. It is historical, like all components of human consciousness. Human self-knowledge is an ongoing "event."

The four gospels indicate Jesus' maturing self-knowledge at certain documented points in his life. Prominent among these were the incident in the temple when he was twelve, his baptism at age thirty, the miracle at Cana, and, perhaps a year or so later, the dramatic awareness of his redemptive destiny. This last was the resolve of that internal moment when "*he began* to teach them that the Son of Man *must* suffer many things, and be rejected by the elders and chief priests and scribes, and be killed, and after three days rise again. He spoke this word openly" (Mark 8:31–32, emphasis added).

It is time, now, to examine two early scenes that disclosed Jesus' growing self-awareness.

2

TWO CONVERSATIONS

I⊤ IS SURELY SIGNIFICANT THAT THE EVANGELIST LUKE, affirming that "Jesus increased in wisdom," placed that affirmation immediately after a revealing comment about Mary: "His mother continued to keep all these things in her heart" (2:51–52).[1]

There is a subtle hint in this juxtaposition. Luke seems to imply that the sustained contemplation in Mary's heart was in some way related to her son's increase in wisdom. The author paints here a provocative picture of the home in Nazareth where Jesus and his mother, joined in a common faith during the three decades of their shared life, continued to mature spiritually in each other's company.

Given the delicacy of this subject, it is important not to sail off into speculations beyond the data provided by Holy Scripture. Does the Bible give any sign of this personal and interpersonal growth of Jesus and his mother? As it touches their relationship—especially their shared faith in the Father's purpose and the mission of the Holy Spirit—is it possible to discern in the relevant biblical texts some indication of this spiritual development? I believe it is.

It is reasonable to begin with the only two recorded conversations between Jesus and his mother. The first, narrated by Luke

(2:41–52), took place in the temple, when Jesus was twelve—the incident when he was lost in Jerusalem for three days and then was found.

The second conversation, reported by John (2:1–11), happened at the wedding feast in Cana of Galilee, apparently when Jesus was about thirty (cf. Luke 3:23). According to this story, Mary approached her son—now a mature man—with an implied request on behalf of some embarrassed newlyweds. Both stories are well-known to readers of the Gospels, so neither needs to be told here in detail.

Luke's source for the first story was, it would appear, Mary herself, whereas in the second instance, John mentions several witnesses, any of whom may have been his source. It is arguable, moreover, that the event at Cana was inscribed in John's personal memory (John 2:2, 11). Since I propose to compare these two gospel accounts, which describe events roughly eighteen years apart, I first mention the reliability of these firsthand sources in order to establish the historicity of the two occasions.

As we compare these two stories, it is important not to overlook a basic fact, which, though almost too obvious at first, may be a bit subtle in its significance: each narrative comes down to us from a different author. That is to say, the elements we may find common to the two accounts are not derived from the thematic perspective of a single writer. The similarities between them are rooted not in a schematic literary presentation but in the recollection of real historical events.

Indeed, with respect to each author's theological intent, the two stories are decidedly different: Luke, along with his pervading and characteristic interest in the symbolism of the temple, tells the story of finding Jesus in specific terms he will later take up in his account of the Lord's third-day resurrection. In this respect, it is significant that Luke introduces this conversation by mentioning the Passover

(Luke 2:41). John, on the other hand, is preoccupied with his own theological motif: the seven "signs" that provide narrative structure to Jesus' public ministry. The wedding feast of Cana is the first of these signs (John 2:11).

PARALLEL STRUCTURES

Notwithstanding these literary and interpretive differences, Luke's and John's stories share striking points of similarity that should prompt us to compare them:

First, each conversation between Jesus and Mary is recorded in direct address; they are both explicitly *quoted*. Luke and John provide us with at least substantial approximations of their words.

Second, in each encounter between them, Jesus asks his mother a question: "Why did you seek me? Did you not know that I must be about the things of my Father?" *and* "What does your concern have to do with me?" These questions to Mary do not function as inquiries; they are directed, rather, to *ending* the conversation, not prolonging it.

It is surely significant that Mary, neither time, answers her son. What she *does*, however, is very different in the two cases, and, I will argue, this difference is related to their spiritual growth and understanding.

Third, both stories are told from Mary's perspective, not from Jesus'. Thus, when the twelve-year-old boy is lost in the temple for three days, the narrator simply leaves him there, while the story line continues with Mary and Joseph.

A parallel perspective is found in the story of the wedding feast of Cana. John begins by observing, "The mother of Jesus was there." Only then does he mention, "Now both Jesus and his disciples were invited to the wedding." Likewise, the initiative in this account is taken—and then sustained—by Mary. In this first of his signs, wherein he "manifested his glory," Jesus is said to act only at his mother's initiative.

Fourth, and, I believe, most important, these two narratives share a common feature of psychology difficult to label. I am hesitant to call it "contention" because this word often conveys a tone of belligerence or disrespect. However we name it, nonetheless, both stories—in the temple at Jerusalem and at the wedding party in Cana—portray Jesus and his mother as "not agreed." They are not in harmony. The two conversations convey, between Mary and her son, a sense of initial opposition. Their questions to each other disclose a rough patch, as it were, a foothold of friction that serves to move the narrative forward.

To appreciate this quality, we can easily construct alternative narratives that would demonstrate the difference. Let us suppose, for instance, that when Mary asked Jesus, "Son, why have you done this to us? Look, your father and I have sought you anxiously," he answered, "Oh, how embarrassing. Terribly sorry, I'm sure. Distracted, you understand, with these rabbinical questions, I lost all sense of time. I do promise it won't happen in the future."

Or again, when Mary mentioned, "They have no wine," let us imagine that Jesus responded, "Good heavens! I failed to notice. Thank you so much for bringing this to my attention. Let me see what can be done about the problem."

In neither conjecture, obviously, would there be much of a story. In other words, the patch of personal friction between Jesus and his mother provides the narrative foothold for the two stories to advance.

It is in this fourth point of comparison that we observe an essential difference between the two accounts: their endings.

In the first case, when Jesus is twelve years old, his question to Mary is literally the last word in the conversation: "Did you not know that I must be about the things of my Father?" Jesus thus breaks off the dialogue. His question, Luke tells us, leaves Mary and

Joseph confused and speechless: "But they did not understand the statement which he spoke to them."

In the later scene at Cana, however, Mary's response to her son is dramatically different: Here it is *she* who breaks off the dialogue. Mary turns away and takes resolute charge of the situation, instructing the servants, "Do whatever he tells you." It is the impulse of her action that precipitates the "beginning of signs that Jesus did." Her dramatically different response, revealing the spiritual growth of the eighteen intervening years, shows that Jesus and his mother have most surely changed . . . and so has their relationship.

Now we may examine each story more closely.

LITTLE BOY LOST

Although the story of Jesus lost and found in the temple is chiefly significant for its Christological import, its narrative structure, as I remarked before, conveys the "action" through the eyes and understanding of Mary. Luke invites us to take this approach in his final comment: "His mother continued to keep all these things in her heart." Indeed, unless the reader approaches the story through Mary's perception, he will miss much of its drama.

We observe, first, that the *lostness* in the story is objective: Jesus is not lost in the sense that he does not know where he is, but in the sense that he is *missing*—his mother does not know where he is. We readers, too, part company with Jesus in this scene: until his parents find him, *we* don't know where he is either. The story's movement is advanced by what Mary and Joseph do:

> When they had finished the days, as they returned, the boy Jesus
> lingered behind in Jerusalem. And Joseph and his mother did not
> know; but supposing him to have been in the company, they went
> a day's journey, and sought him among relatives and friends. So

when they did not find him, they returned to Jerusalem, seeking
Him. (Luke 2:43–45)

The narrative action, taking us readers along with it, first moves
north. The storyteller and his readers travel toward Galilee with
Mary and Joseph. The Evangelist speaks of their worried search,
though he does not directly mention their anxiety—indeed, it is
made explicit only by Mary herself in the closing dialogue (Luke
2:48)—because the anxiety is implied in the details of the search.

Not finding the boy Jesus after a day's journey, Mary and Joseph
return south to Jerusalem—and we go back with them, of course—
to continue their pursuit in the same place they last saw Jesus:

> Now so it was that after three days they found him in the temple,
> sitting in the midst of the teachers, both listening to them and
> asking them questions. (2:46)

Jesus, we all discover, is the center of attention: "And all who
heard him were astonished at his understanding and answers."

The boy's parents are bewildered: "So when they saw him," writes
Luke, "they were amazed." Every parent comprehends their amazement: This was the child they had raised for a dozen years. Yet he did
not accompany them back home after the Passover, as he had done on
every prior trip. Mary and Joseph search for him frantically, but even
when they find him, the child displays not the slightest remorse or
concern for their anxiety. The mother of Jesus finds this insouciance
on the part of her twelve-year-old a bit more than she is disposed to
accept without complaint: "Son, why have you done this to us? Look,
your father and I have sought you anxiously" (Luke 2:48).

Then, the boy, instead of apologizing and promising it will not
happen again, turns the question back on his mother: "Why did you
seek me? Did you not know that I must be about the things of my

Father?" From any other twelve-year-old, this kind of answer would be called "back talk" and treated as impertinent.

I suspect, by the by, that Jesus' answer to Mary was a sort of continuation of his discussion with the rabbis. Recall that Jesus, when his parents discover him in the temple, has been engaged (for three days, apparently) in discourses with the rabbis; he has been asking them questions and answering theirs. In other words, Jesus has been engaged in a pedagogical and rhetorical method where a favored device is the "counterquestion"—the answering of a question by a further and more probing inquiry. We find this style of debate frequently in rabbinic literature and in the Gospels.

The boy Jesus, then, so recently exposed to this pedagogical and rhetorical method here in the temple, spontaneously has recourse to it in order to answer his mother. When she inquires, "*Why* have you done this?" He responds with a counterquestion, "*Why* did you seek me? Did you not know?"

As a matter of fact, Mary did not know, nor did she and Joseph find much reassurance in this brief dialogue with Jesus. Luke tells us, "But they did not understand the statement which he spoke to them" (2:50). Then, the three of them return to Nazareth—in silence, one suspects.

Mary is portrayed as "anxious"—her own word—amazed, and confused. Considered from her perspective—as Luke clearly intends—the story is most noticeable as a test of Mary's faith.

The angel Gabriel had spoken to her nearly thirteen years earlier, when she was little more than half of her present age; she may not have been much older than Jesus was when they found him in the temple.[2] From that day when the angel visited her, it appears, Mary has understood rather little of what transpired. Like Abraham her forefather, she followed God's will in faith but could hardly guess where it was all leading. She walked obediently, day by day, not knowing whither she went.

Luke's story, which chronicles Jesus' growth in wisdom, is told here through the person who witnessed that growth and who was obliged, in a very personal way, to explore its meaning. It was certainly from her that Luke learned the facts of the case.

A WEDDING AT CANA

The miracle at Cana, narrated in a story unique to John (2:1–11), apparently took place shortly after Jesus' forty-day fast in the wilderness. About that time and—it would seem—subsequent to the arrest of John the Baptist, "Jesus came to Galilee, preaching the gospel of the kingdom."[3] One of the villages in Galilee was Cana.

Although the sequence in John's early chapters is notoriously difficult to accommodate to the chronology of the other gospels, he does indicate that Jesus visited Cana *after* the calling of the first disciples[4] and *prior to* the larger ministry at Capernaum.[5]

The circumstances of Jesus' visit are not too difficult to imagine: Traveling north, he arrived first at his mother's home at Nazareth, nine miles south of Cana. He was accompanied by his earliest followers, one of whom was Nathaniel, a man who actually hailed from Cana (John 21:2–3).

Although now and then a regional rivalry between Nazareth and Cana prompted the citizens of one village to disparage the merits of the other (John 1:46), we are probably right to think such banter benign. The two places were doubtless linked—along with neighboring Bethsaida (1:41–45)—by numerous friendships, and we know that Jesus visited Cana more than once (4:46).

It is hardly surprising, therefore, that Mary was invited to a wedding in that village. Indeed, John begins his story by noting *her* presence there (John 2:1). Nor is it extravagant to imagine she may have gone to Cana early in order to assist with the preparations.

At least, this would reasonably explain why John separates

her presence in Cana from the invitation extended to Jesus and his disciples. More than one reader has gained the impression that Jesus and his friends, newly arrived at Nazareth, may have been something of an afterthought on the Cana guest list. In turn, this sudden influx of extra visitors may explain why, during the course of the celebration, the wine ran short!

If—as I guess—Mary assisted in the wedding preparations, it is not surprising that it was she who noticed the wine shortage. Indeed, during the several days of feasting, this helpful wedding guest may occasionally have cast a wary eye at the beverage supply, growing a tad alarmed at its steady decline. At last it was gone, and Mary determined to speak with her son.

What prompted the mother of Jesus to take this step? What did she expect? John does not say, and Mary's actual expectation remains one of the genuine mysteries of the story.

This does not mean, however, that we are totally at sea on the matter. We do know the substance of a message Mary received from an angel more than thirty years earlier:

> And behold, you will conceive in your womb and bring forth
> a Son, and shall call his name Jesus. He will be great, and will
> be called the Son of the Highest . . . therefore, also, that Holy
> One who is to be born will be called the Son of God. (Luke
> 1:31–32, 35)

Moreover, the birth and infant life of Jesus were attended by extraordinary, even miraculous, circumstances.[6] In addition, Mary had heard her son—from tender years—speak of God as "my Father" (Luke 2:49).

How did Mary understand all these things? It is not at all clear that she *did* understand. At least, it would be silly to suppose that she thought of Jesus in formal creedal terms.

Mary's knowledge of Jesus was not of this dogmatic sort. It was, first of all, a mother's knowledge of her child, especially a child who had lived with her well into adulthood.

There was surely more, as well: it would be wrong to imagine that when the Holy Spirit, "the power of the Highest," descended upon her to effect the conception of Jesus, the Spirit intended this descent as a transitory visit.

Mary was not just a temporary or purely physical conduit of the Incarnation. The relationship between Jesus and his mother was transpersonal and transcendent to biology. She was truly the mother, and not simply the "bearer," of God's Son. When, during her pregnancy, she declared, "He who is mighty has done great things for me" (Luke 1:49), she was aware of at least this much. Day by day she measured, and now continued to measure, what this meant. If she knew Jesus at all, if being the *mother* of God's Son meant *anything*, then it certainly meant she was entitled to speak to him about a shortage of wine.

THE WOMAN AND THE HOUR

As Mary approached her son at Cana, her sole concern was the welfare of those who sponsored the wedding feast. She does not seem to have had anything more specific in mind. This impression is conveyed, I believe, in what she eventually says to the waiters: "Do *whatever* he tells you." This "whatever" (Greek *ho ti*) perfectly sums up her concern. Mary does not request a miracle; she simply wants the problem dealt with, and she trusts Jesus to do it.

Indeed, as the story begins, there is nothing to suggest a miracle is about to happen. John's account is far removed from the fabulous atmosphere of later apocryphal literature, such as the *Infancy Gospel of Thomas*, which tells of various prodigies worked by the boy Jesus: breathing life into clay birds, stretching a piece of timber to help

Joseph finish constructing a bed, even striking a playmate dead and blinding the child's parents!

There is nothing of this sort in Holy Scripture, where the Cana miracle is identified as Jesus' "beginning of signs." This "beginning," I believe, may be understood in two nonexclusive ways: The reference has a literary significance, meaning that the Cana miracle was the first of the specific seven "signs" narrated by John. The word *beginning* also means here an historical fact: this was the initial miracle actually performed by Jesus.

In truth, the other gospels record no miracles until Jesus' slightly later ministry in Capernaum.[7] In short, Jesus has done nothing, so far, that would prompt Mary to expect a miraculous response to her solicitous comment, "They have no wine."

Jesus' response has been variously translated, but I believe the New King James effort best conveys its sense: "Woman, what does your concern have to do with me? My hour has not yet come." Two aspects of this response are in order:

First, it is important to eliminate a hint of harshness conveyed in the translation—to wit, in English it is not usually considered polite to address someone as "Woman." However, the underlying idiom, the Aramaic word used by Jesus—'anot'a—was a formal and even decorous manner of address. Indeed, this is how Jesus habitually speaks to women in the Gospels, including a Canaanite petitioner (Matthew 15:28), a crippled woman in the synagogue (Luke 13:12), the Samaritan woman at the well (John 4:21), the woman accused of adultery (8:10), and Mary Magdalene at the tomb (20:13). Perhaps our English "ma'am" comes closest to the sense of the Aramaic idiom.

It is especially noteworthy that in John's gospel Jesus addresses his mother this way as he is dying (John 19:26). In this gospel, Cana and Calvary are the only places where Mary's son speaks to her, and the same word is used both times.

Second, Jesus explains his reluctance by adding, "My hour has not yet come." This reference to the "hour" is important in Johannine theology, where it designates the elected time of Jesus' glorification. On the eve of his sufferings and death, Jesus prays, "Father, the *hour* has come. Glorify Your Son, that Your Son also may glorify You" (John 17:1). This is the imminent hour of which he says, "The *hour* is coming, yes, has now come."[8]

These considerations of Jesus' "hour" in Johannine theology, however, are not entirely pertinent to the historical context under consideration. We are treating Jesus' mother here as a real person, not just a character in a work of theological literature. Our immediate question is: How did this historical Mary, in that actual moment at Cana, understand Jesus' words, "My hour has not yet come"?

In that context, the words could only have meant, "It's not time yet." That is to say, Jesus was declining his mother's suggestion that he intervene in the wine problem. *De facto*, he was telling her no.

And how does Mary respond to his objection? She ignores it! Mary does not argue the point with her son. She simply turns and boldly says to the waiters, "Do whatever he tells you." She thus puts the pressure squarely on her son, manifestly confident that he will not disappoint her.

It is worth remarking that "Do whatever he tells you" are Mary's last recorded words.

We know the day's outcome: Mary's son, at the direct instigation of his mother, transformed the water into wine. We surmise, too, that the wedding party was transformed, once the guests discovered that the host had "kept the good wine until now!"

Indeed, Jesus' own ministry was transformed. Here it was that he "manifested his glory; and his disciples believed in him." The "signs" have begun.

Up to this point, it was possible for their contemporaries to think of Jesus and John the Baptist mainly in terms of similarity, inasmuch as both were teachers. No more, however, because "John performed no sign" (John 10:41). After the Cana event, people in the region would tell "how God anointed Jesus of Nazareth with the Holy Spirit and with power, who went about doing good" (Acts 10:38).

In these two stories from the Bible, we are able to trace at least a fraction in the outline of a spiritual and psychological development. This trace strengthens our sense that God's eternal Word assumed not only our human nature—considered abstractly and in general—but the concrete, historical circumstances of an individual human life. He made himself a subjective participant in human history, someone whose existence and experience were circumscribed by the limiting conditions of time and space—before and after, here and there, then and now. The organic particularity of Jesus' life included a bit of overt pressure from his mother.

The doctrine of the Incarnation affirms that we were redeemed through the personal experiences of God's Son in human history—the very things that the Word underwent—from the instant of his conception, through his birth and infancy, through the events and phases of his life, through his tears and laughter, through his ministry and teaching, through his obedient sufferings and death on the cross, through his resurrection and entry into eternal glory. Human redemption "happened" in the humanity of the eternal Word as he passed through, transformed, and deified our existence.

"Imagine," Augustine wrote of Jesus,

that the Almighty did not create this man—however he was formed—from the womb of his mother, but abruptly introduced him before our eyes. Suppose he passed through no ages from infancy to youth, or that he neither ate nor slept. Would that not have proved the heretics correct?[9]

An adequate Christology, then, affirms that the Word's becoming flesh refers to more than the single instant of his becoming present in the Virgin's womb. He continued becoming flesh and dwelling among us, in the sense that his assumed body and soul developed and grew through the complex experiences of a particular human life. We see this actually happening in these two conversations between Jesus and his mother.

If a concrete human life was assumed in the Incarnation, Jesus did not simply have a mother; he had *this* mother, to whom he related as a real person, whose influence was crucial to his own development as a human being. She was, like himself, a person of faith. Indeed, her faith pertained very much to his own person and mission.

3

BAPTISM

ACCORDING TO THE CHRONOLOGY SUGGESTED IN THE EAR-
liest apostolic preaching (Acts 1:22), the most ancient accounts of
Jesus' public life began with the story of his baptism, perhaps two
months or so before the miraculous sign at Cana. Having examined
the event at Cana, therefore, we must back up a bit, to reflect on two
events that happened prior to that miracle: Jesus' baptism and his
subsequent temptation in the wilderness.

Unlike the accounts of his childhood in Matthew and Luke,
the story of Jesus' baptism was part of the earliest apostolic preaching. We are certain of this because that preaching was based on a
defined narrative structure, which invariably began with John the
Baptist.

We discern that established structure and sequence in the preaching patterns in the Acts of the Apostles. Thus, when the apostle Peter
began to evangelize Cornelius and his friends at Caesarea, he commenced his story by speaking of the ministry of John the Baptist:

> That word you know, which was proclaimed throughout all
> Judea, and began from Galilee after the baptism which John

29

preached—how God anointed Jesus of Nazareth with the Holy Spirit and with power. (Acts 10:37–38)

The same starting point of Jesus' ministry is discerned in the apostle Paul's evangelization of Pisidian Antioch. To tell his audience of Jesus, Paul began by linking him directly to the ministry of John:

God raised up for Israel a Savior—Jesus—after John had first preached, before his coming, the baptism of repentance to all the people of Israel. (Acts 13:23–24)

In short, the "evangelical narrative"—the narrative form in which the apostles first proclaimed the gospel—embraced the events of Jesus' life, *beginning with* the baptism by John the Baptist.

Now this is exactly what we should expect, from the earlier directive Peter gave to the assembled apostles prior to the Pentecostal outpouring of the Holy Spirit. When they determined, at that time, to choose some person to take the place of Judas Iscariot to fill up the number of the twelve witnesses, Peter specified the time period concerning which the chosen person would have to bear witness. He must be selected, said Peter, from among "these men who have accompanied us all the time that the Lord Jesus went in and out among us, *beginning from the baptism by John* to the day that he was taken up from us" (Acts 1:21–22, emphasis added).

That period of time, beginning with John's ministry, defined the specified limits of the original apostolic narrative, the primitive story structure of the gospel.

JOHN THE BAPTIST

The significance of John's ministry with respect to the gospel prompted Luke to introduce the Baptist's appearance with considerable solemnity, fixing its setting within general history:

Now in the fifteenth year of the reign of Tiberius Caesar, Pontius Pilate being governor of Judea, Herod being tetrarch of Galilee, his brother Philip tetrarch of Iturea and the region of Trachonitis, and Lysanias tetrarch of Abilene, while Annas and Caiaphas were high priests, the word of God came to John the son of Zacharias in the wilderness. And he went into the whole region around the Jordan, preaching a baptism of repentance for the remission of sins. (Luke 3:1–3)

Although we learn some few details of John's moral and social teaching from Matthew (3:7–9) and Luke (3:10–17), most of the New Testament's interest in John is based on his relationship to Jesus.[1] All the New Testament sources speak of Jesus' superiority to John, and only Luke indicates that Jesus and John were biologically related through their mothers (Luke 1:36).

As described by Mark, John receives Jesus among the multitude coming to be baptized:

Then all the land of Judea, and those from Jerusalem, went out to him and were all baptized by him in the Jordan River, confessing their sins. (Mark 1:5)

Matthew's account of this scene includes a brief discussion between Jesus and John, just prior to the baptism:

Then Jesus came from Galilee to John at the Jordan to be baptized by him. And John tried to prevent him, saying, "I need to be baptized by you, and are you coming to me?" But Jesus answered and said to him, "Permit it to be so now, for thus it is fitting for us to fulfill all righteousness." Then he allowed him. (Matthew 3:13–15)

This hesitation on John's part serves, once again, to emphasize Jesus' superiority to John. Because this baptism was a sign of repentance, John himself sensed an incongruity in Jesus' submission to it. Nonetheless, Jesus accepts this service at John's hand, "to fulfill all righteousness." Recognizing John's baptism to come from God (Matthew 21:23–27), Jesus gives it his public endorsement. In submitting to it, the Sinless One places himself among the sinners he came to redeem.

BAPTISMAL PRAYER

In the story of Jesus' baptism, the variations among the Evangelists come mainly from their differing lines of interest.

In Matthew, for instance, the scene is portrayed as a theophany, a revelation given to the bystanders: "*This* is My beloved Son, in whom I am well pleased" (Matthew 3:17, emphasis added). Matthew very soon strengthens this emphasis by his insertion of Isaiah 9:1–2, a text about the revelation of the divine light to the nations (Matthew 4:13–16). This emphasis is related to Matthew's theme of universal evangelization.

This baptismal revelation in Matthew is Trinitarian: the Father is revealed in the voice from heaven, the Son in the person baptized in the Jordan, and the Holy Spirit in the descending dove. In a parallel to this baptismal revelation, given at the beginning of Jesus' ministry, Matthew places a corresponding "baptismal" scene at the end of it. This one is also Trinitarian: "Go therefore and make disciples of all the nations, baptizing them in the name of the Father and of the Son and of the Holy Spirit" (Matthew 28:19).

In Mark and Luke, on the other hand, Jesus' baptism is described, not in public and theophanic terms, but as his personal encounter with his Father. Instead of Matthew's "this is," Mark and Luke give us direct address: "*You* are." "*You* are my beloved Son, in *you* I am well pleased" (Mark 1:11; Luke 3:22).[2] In Mark and Luke, the accent is on Jesus' own spiritual experience.

In fact, Mark does not indicate that anyone else present even saw the dove: "And immediately, coming up out of the water, *he saw* the heavens parting and the Spirit descending upon him like a dove" (Mark 1:10, emphasis added).[3]

This brings us to Luke, whose account of Jesus' baptism is contained in a single, condensed, and tightly constructed sentence:

> Now it happened, when all the people were baptized, and Jesus—having been baptized—was praying, that heaven was opened, and the Holy Spirit, in bodily form like a dove, came down upon Him, and there was a voice from heaven: "*You* are My beloved Son; in *You* I am well pleased." (3:21–22)

In Luke's account, six details of the baptism seem especially worthy of attention:

First, John the Baptist is not mentioned in the scene at all; Luke, having already spoken of John's arrest (Luke 3:20), leaves him out of the baptismal story completely.

Second, the baptism itself is not Luke's central concern. Indeed, it has already happened and is mentioned only in a subordinate expression: "*having been* baptized." Luke's focus is directed, not to the baptism, but to Jesus' *experience* of the Father and the Holy Spirit.

Third, Jesus' baptism is not isolated from that of the other people: "when all the people were baptized." The Evangelist's stress on this point indicates Jesus' solidarity with the rest of humanity.

This emphasis is important to Luke's theology of the Incarnation. In the immediate context, Jesus' organic solidarity with the human race is addressed by Luke's inclusion—immediately after the baptism—of the Savior's genealogy, in which his ancestry is traced all the way back to Adam (Luke 3:23–38). In other words, the mention of "the people" in this baptismal scene pertains to Luke's larger interest in the humanity of Jesus: he is at one with the whole human race, descended from the fallen Adam.

Fourth, only Luke speaks of the Savior at prayer in the baptismal story: "Jesus—having been baptized—*was praying.*" This is the first of many times Luke describes Jesus communing with God as other human beings commune with God—namely, by prayer.[4] Luke often accents prayer in Jesus' life, something we will explore in full in a later chapter.[5]

Fifth, Luke emphasizes the visible way the Holy Spirit descended on Jesus: "the Holy Spirit, in *bodily form* [*somatiko eidei*] like a dove, came down upon him" (3:22).

Although Luke has already made the activity of the Holy Spirit thematic in his version of the gospel,[6] a particular theological note attends the Spirit's appearance here in the baptismal scene—namely, the baptism is portrayed as Jesus' public *anointing* by the Holy Spirit. Jesus will soon speak of this "anointing" when, in the first words of his public ministry—and quoting the book of Isaiah—he announces, "The Spirit of the Lord is upon me, / Because He has anointed me" (4:18; Isaiah 61:1).

The Spirit's baptismal anointing of Jesus is theologically decisive for Luke. It is, in fact, the chronological starting point of the apostolic message (cf. Acts 1:21–22). In respect to Jesus' baptismal anointing, moreover, Luke will later quote St. Peter's assertion that the gospel itself

> began from Galilee after the baptism which John preached: how God *anointed* Jesus of Nazareth with the Holy Spirit and with power, who went about doing good and healing all who were oppressed by the devil, for God was with him. (Acts 10:37–38, emphasis added)

Sixth, in Luke's version of the baptism—as in Mark's—the voice of the Father addresses Jesus *directly.* It does so twice: "*You* are my beloved Son; in you *I* am well pleased."[7] We take note of the vigorously repeated *I/you* structure.

The proclamation of Jesus' sonship hardly comes as news to Luke's readers, of course, who recall the announcement of Gabriel to Mary:

> The Holy Spirit will come upon you, and the power of the Highest will overshadow you; therefore, also, that Holy One who is to be born will be called the Son of God. (Luke 1:35)

Let us insist that this experience of identification did not come to Jesus as "fresh information." The Father's word here should not be understood as Jesus' "calling," in the sense familiar to the Hebrew prophets. Jesus already *knew* he was called, and he already knew the identity of his Father. Eighteen years earlier, he had asked his parents, "Why did you seek me? Did you not know that I must be about *the things of my Father?*" (Luke 2:49, emphasis added).

In the baptism, the Father's voice expresses, rather, a heightened reassurance to Jesus, the sign that his ministry should now begin. As the apostle Peter remarked of this scene, "God was with him" (Acts 10:38). The Father's word is the encouraging answer to Jesus' prayer at the baptism. It conveys the Father's presence and loving approval. In short, Luke's version of the baptism lays the accent on Jesus' personal experience of communion with his Father, a communion sustained right up to the death scene, where Jesus twice invokes God as "Father" (Luke 23:34, 46).

A MORE AMPLE MESSAGE

A closer attention to the "voice from heaven" suggests further aspects of the baptismal experience of Jesus.

For example, when the Father addressed him as "beloved Son"

and declared himself "well pleased," these expressions were not entirely—if the word be allowed—*original*. On the contrary, these words doubtless evoked in the Savior's mind two biblical texts, with which he was already familiar from those years of study in the synagogue. It is important to consider them in detail.

The first Old Testament text recorded the electrifying word spoken by God to Abraham:

> Take now your son, your only one, Isaac, *whom you love*, and go to the land of Moriah, and offer him there as a burnt offering on one of the mountains of which I shall tell you. (Genesis 22:2, emphasis added)

The memory of this dramatic story, evoked by the "voice from heaven," beckoned Jesus—at the moment of his baptism—to assume in his own life the sacrificial role of Isaac. Thus, at the very beginning of his ministry, Jesus was already summoned to consider the coming tragic events that would, in due course, put an end to it. Prior to proclaiming a single word of the gospel, he received an early intimation of the mystery of the cross.

The implicit reference to Isaac and Abraham in the baptismal scene is even more apparent if we consider the Greek (Septuagint) version of Genesis 22:2, where the Hebrew word for "only" (*yahid*) is changed to "beloved" (*agapetos*): "Take your *beloved* son, whom you *love* . . ."

Nothing in this story of his baptism compels us to imagine that Jesus, at that moment, grasped the complete meaning of his correspondence to Isaac. Although we readers are aware of Simeon's earlier prophecy of the cross (Luke 2:34–35), the Evangelist gives no indication that Jesus knew of it. Nor has the Savior yet encountered the homicidal hostility of those enemies to whom the gospel came as a threat. Consequently, it is reasonable to suppose that the full inference of his likeness to Isaac took time to grow in the mind of Jesus, as events unfolded over the next couple of years.

We know this did happen, however. Once the murderous plot against him became alarmingly apparent, Jesus recalled that image of Isaac, and he invited his adversaries to consider it in the context of their own treachery. To these enemies, priding themselves as "Abraham's descendants," Jesus asserted, "Your father Abraham rejoiced to see my day, and he saw and was glad." To the opponents of the gospel, Jesus thus identified himself as the true Isaac, whose promised arrival inspired the joy—the laughter!—of ancient Abraham (cf. Genesis 17:17). It was for this assertion—and for his further claim to antecede the days of Abraham—that Jesus' enemies "took up stones to throw at him" (John 8:37–59).

A second biblical text, also familiar to Jesus, was evoked by the "voice from heaven" at the baptism. This one came from the book of Isaiah and introduced the mysterious appearance of God's Suffering Servant. Indeed, this passage stands at the beginning of the Isaian Servant Songs: "Behold! My Servant whom I uphold; / My soul delights in My chosen one. / I have put My Spirit upon him" (42:1).

Although I have quoted this prophecy as it appears in the transmitted Hebrew (Masoretic) text, the early Christians were familiar with another version of it, a Greek translation closer to the Aramaic words Jesus heard at his baptism. Matthew quotes the passage thus:

> Behold! My Servant whom I have chosen,
> My beloved [agapetos] in whom My soul is well pleased!
> I will put My Spirit upon him. (Matthew 12:18)

Thus, even as the Holy Spirit descends on Jesus and the Father's voice addresses him as "Son," the vocabulary of the scene recalls the loyal Servant from the book of Isaiah, the image that will largely determine, as time goes on, Jesus' own understanding of his role in the mystery of redemption.

By the juxtaposition of these two texts, the Father's Son and the true Isaac is identified as God's Servant, in whom he is well pleased. More and more, as the events of his life unfold—especially the conspiracy of his adversaries—Jesus will sound the depths of that identification. In relentlessly straight lines, both images—Isaac and the Suffering Servant—point in the direction of the cross.

In the experience of his baptism, then, Jesus received an earnest intimation of what that baptism ultimately symbolized. Luke will take up this motif in the later scene, where Jesus foretells the strife and divisions attendant on the proclamation of the gospel: "I have a baptism to be baptized with, and how distressed I am till it is accomplished!" (12:50; cf. Mark 10:38).

CALLING THE DISCIPLES

According to the fourth gospel, the first followers of Jesus were drawn from the disciples of John the Baptist. They apparently came to know Jesus in the context of his own baptism by John. Since John the Evangelist does not narrate the story of Jesus' temptations in the wilderness, the exact chronology of the call of the disciples is far from clear. The Synoptics do not mention the calling until after the temptation accounts.

The fourth gospel not only omits the temptation story; it also does not even explicitly record Jesus' baptism. Nonetheless, there is an unmistakable reference to it in what John the Baptist said about Jesus:

I saw the Spirit descending from heaven like a dove, and it remained upon him. I did not know him, but He who sent me to baptize with water said to me, "Upon whom you see the Spirit descending, and remaining on him, this is he who baptizes with the Holy Spirit." And I have seen and testified that this is the Son of God. (John 1:32–34)

At that time, John the Baptist spoke of Jesus not only as "the Son of God" but also as "the Lamb of God who takes away the sin of the world" (John 1:29). Inspired to curiosity (at least) by these mysterious references, two of John's disciples began to follow Jesus as he was walking. Noticing this, he inquired what they wanted. "Where are you staying?" they asked. "Come and see," he answered, and "they came and saw where he was staying, and remained with him that day (now it was about the tenth hour)" (1:39).

From the specific detail that they stayed with Jesus until about four o'clock in the afternoon, we are confident that this account comes from an immediate witness, arguably Andrew. The latter, in any case, found his brother, Peter, and introduced him to Jesus. Philip and Nathaniel (probably identical to the "Bartholomew" of the Synoptics[8]) joined the group in quick succession. At least seven of the growing group were fishermen (cf. John 21:2); another was a tax collector (Mark 2:14). All of them appear to have been from Galilee.

When these men were originally called, they could hardly guess how their lives would change. First, sharing the lot of someone who had no place to rest his head (Matthew 8:20), they wandered with him all over Galilee and with him sailed on fishing boats to towns and villages all around the Sea of Tiberias, assisting his ministry in various ways, such as baptizing new followers.

When Jesus dispatched them, in pairs, to other places, the ministry of these men was an extension of his own, inasmuch as he "gave them power over unclean spirits" (Mark 6:7). Consequently, "they went out and preached repentance. And they cast out many demons, and anointed with oil many who were sick, and healed them" (Mark 6:12–13).

These men traveled light, taking "nothing for the journey except a staff—no bag, no bread, no copper in money belts" (6:8). It is not entirely clear how many trips they made this way, nor were these the only men thus sent out. At one point, Jesus "appointed seventy others also, and sent them two by two before his face into every city and place where he himself was about to go" (Luke 10:1).

In due course, the function and purpose of these missionaries changed, just as Jesus' own ministry did. Originally summoned to assist the Savior in the spiritual renewal of Israel, they shared his rejection by Israel's official leaders. Especially during the final year of this ministry, Jesus' followers were reduced to a mere handful, a "little flock" (Luke 12:32).

When it became clear that Jesus would be completely rejected by official Judaism, he began to lay the foundation of a new community, a remnant *qahal* or "congregation" (in Greek, *ekklesia*), united in the foundational confession, "You are the Christ, the Son of the living God" (Matthew 16:16–18).

When the new community, based on this confession, began to take shape, Jesus provided organizational leadership for it. After a night spent praying about this development, the Savior appointed twelve of these men—commonly called "those sent," or apostles—to be the patriarchal foundation stones of the new congregation (Revelation 21:14). As we continue to reflect on Jesus in the flesh, there will be occasion to speak of some of these men, to whose preaching and writing we owe everything we know of him.

A somewhat closer look at the gospel texts also reveals, I think, how Jesus related to these original disciples—even from the beginning—as "individuals," as particular men. He does not permit their specific identities to become lost in the group. Philip, Andrew, Thomas, and the others preserve their individual characters.

Observe, for instance, how he teases them. Jesus' irony toward Nathaniel is a perfect example of this. Observe: Nathaniel speaks his mind. When told about Jesus, Nathaniel asks Philip, "Can anything good come out of Nazareth?" That's pretty plain. No sugarcoating for Nathaniel. Then, how does Jesus react to this candor about his own hometown? He says of Nathaniel, "Here is an Israelite who says what he thinks" (or is "without guile"—in the more respectful translation). Such was the beginning of Nathaniel's friendship with Jesus.

And what shall we say of the nickname Jesus gave to the two sons of Zebedee: James and John? He called them "sons of thunder," which in our modern idiom would be "hotheads." One suspects the brothers received this moniker because of an incident recorded by Luke:

> And as they went, they entered a village of the Samaritans, to prepare for him. But they did not receive him, because his face was set for the journey to Jerusalem. And when his disciples James and John saw this, they said, "Lord, do You want us to command fire to come down from heaven and consume them, just as Elijah did?" (Luke 9:52–54)

In response, Jesus admonishes the two brothers, but their nickname sticks (Mark 3:17).

Luke, who describes the wrath of Zebedee's sons against the Samaritans, also tells the ironic "second half" of the story, when he comes to the Samaritan mission in the Acts of the Apostles. After Philip baptized the Samaritans, Luke tells us, the church at Jerusalem "sent Peter and John to them, who, when they had come down, prayed for them that they might receive the Holy Spirit."[9]

Luke relished the irony of it: John bar Zebedee had wanted fire from heaven to fall on the Samaritans. He got his wish! The church at Jerusalem sent *him*—when the time was right—as one of its delegates to call down on the Samaritans the true fire from heaven—the Holy Spirit.

Most ironic of all is the case of Simon bar Jona ("Simon Johnson"), to whom Jesus assigned the nickname "Rock"—*Cephas* in Aramaic, *Petros* in Greek. This was the disciple who thrice denied even knowing Jesus, after boasting that *he* would never do such a thing. Peter, when he felt enthusiastic, imagined himself invincible, but he fell miserably when his enthusiasm waned. He readily mistook a rush of adrenaline for an outpouring of the Holy Spirit—a confusion rather common among individuals with too much adrenaline. Rock? Jesus surely recognized the name's improbability in Peter's case. The only time this "Rock Johnson" showed any rocklike quality was on that memorable occasion when he attempted to walk on water!

In all these instances, we perceive a light and jocund side of Jesus' relationship with these men, whom he chose "that they might be with Him" (Mark 3:14). With these disciples, Jesus carried himself as a man among men, to whom he was bound by the sorts of habits, attitudes, and discourse in which most normal men establish friendships and maintain loyalties.

4

THE HUMAN CONDITION

WHEN THE NEW TESTAMENT SPEAKS OF THE ETERNAL
Son's assumption of our humanity—his Incarnation, or "enfleshing"—the event is described in terms of a lessening, the embracing
of limitation, even a self-emptying. In witness to this conviction,
a primitive Christian hymn, partly preserved in the epistle to the
Philippians, declared that Jesus Christ

> being in the form of God, did not consider equality with God
> a thing to be seized, but emptied himself [heavton ekenosen],
> assuming the form of a bondservant. (Philippians 2:6–7)

From the beginning, Christians believed that God's Son "less-
ened" himself by becoming human. He "was made a little lower
than the angels, for the suffering of death" (Hebrews 2:9). The act
of becoming a human being necessarily imposed limits on his condition and experience. Paul described this "limitation"—consequent
to the Word's enfleshing—with a metaphor of wealth and poverty.
Thus, he told the Corinthians:

For you know the grace of our Lord Jesus Christ, that though he was rich, yet for your sakes he became poor, that you through his poverty might become rich. (2 Corinthians 8:9)

Servanthood and poverty are metaphors of limitation.[1] They assert that God's Son really did become "one of us." This term, "one of us" (*heis ex hemon*), was favored in the fifth century by Cyril of Alexandria, who used this expression often in his sermons and commentaries on the Gospels, to speak of Jesus' total solidarity with all human beings by reason of the Incarnation.

When we inquire what sorts of limitation God's Son assumed in the Incarnation, it is clear to nearly all readers of the New Testament that certain physical limitations were included. That is to say, if Jesus did not grow tired, how was it he fell sound asleep in the boat? If he did not become thirsty and exhausted, what prompted him to sit down at a well and ask a Samaritan woman for a drink?

These limitations included a range of psychological discomforts. At the death of a beloved friend, for example, "Jesus wept" (John 11:35). Faced with the sustained and repeated infidelities of Jerusalem, "He saw the city and wept over it" (Luke 19:41). Some experiences left him with the feelings of utter exasperation: "O faithless generation, how long shall I be with you? How long shall I bear with you?" (Mark 9:19). At the worst experience of all, he cried out, "My God, my God, why have You forsaken me?" (Mark 15:34).

If the eternal Word's taking of our humanity made him vulnerable to emotional pain, it also rendered him susceptible to temptation. When, after fasting for forty days, he grew hungry, it is hardly surprising that an early first temptation was related to food (Matthew 4:3; Luke 4:3). Adequate attention to Jesus *in the flesh* can hardly omit those temptations to which the flesh is heir. Holy Scripture, at least, does not omit them.

This aspect of the Incarnation was nowhere more emphatically asserted than in the epistle to the Hebrews, which says of Jesus:

> Therefore, in all things he had to be made like his brothers,
> that he might be a merciful and faithful High Priest in the
> things of God, to make atonement for the sins of the people.
> For in that he himself has suffered, *being tempted*, he is able
> to aid those who are tempted. (Hebrews 2:17–18, emphasis
> added)

For the earliest Christians, the temptations of Jesus were at once the expression of his full humanity and the encouraging evidence of his ability to sympathize with the trials faced by those who put their trust in him:

> For we do not have a High Priest who cannot sympathize with
> our weaknesses, but was in everything *tempted as we are*, yet
> without sin. (Hebrews 4:15, emphasis added)

MARK

The temptations Jesus faced, however, were not simply based on his being human. They came also from demonic intrusion, like the temptations of other human beings.

It is not known when (or if) a narrative of Jesus' temptations in the wilderness became a standard part in the narrative sequence of the apostolic proclamation—it is not mentioned, for example, in the Acts of the Apostles—but we do find it in its earliest literary form, namely, the gospel of Mark. Immediately following Jesus' baptism, Mark informs us,

> The Spirit drove him into the wilderness. And he was there in
> the wilderness forty days, tempted by Satan, and was with the
> wild beasts; and the angels ministered to him. (Mark 1:12–13)

Even these few details of Mark's brief narrative convey a considerable amount of its theology:

First, the Holy Spirit, who has come down upon Jesus at his baptism, now "drives" him into the wilderness. As we shall observe, all three accounts of Jesus' temptation include this detail about the Holy Spirit. All of them agree that his experience of the Holy Spirit prompted Jesus to go into the desert to face "the Tempter"—*ho Peirazon* (Matthew 4:3).

Second, for Mark there was a pastoral significance in the fact that Jesus' trial in the wilderness followed immediately on his baptism. That significance arose from the recognition that Christians, in *their* baptism, enacted a ritual replication of Israel's passage through the Red Sea in the Exodus. After that "baptismal" passage, the Israelites experienced various temptations in the wilderness. The apostle Paul, speaking of those ancient partakers of the Exodus, wrote that "all our fathers were under the cloud, all passed through the sea, all were baptized with Moses in the cloud and in the sea" (1 Corinthians 10:1–2).

After that Exodus baptism, Paul went on, those primitive forefathers journeyed out to the wilderness, where they experienced temptation. The apostle, reminding his readers that the Israelites did not fare well in those temptations (1 Corinthians 1:5–10), proceeded to draw a practical lesson for the Christian life:

> Now these things happened to them as examples, and they were
> written for *our* admonition, upon whom the ends of the ages
> have come. (1 Corinthians 10:11, emphasis added)

That is to say, after their baptisms, Christians—and particularly the Corinthians!—were also going to be tempted. They must expect it, but they must also be assured that

> no temptation has overtaken you except *what is human*; but God
> is faithful, who will not allow you to be tempted beyond what
> you are able. (1 Corinthians 10:13, emphasis added)

Paul insists here that Christians must not imagine they will escape the experience of such temptation that is "human"—*anthropinos*. (The fact that temptation is demonic does not make it less human.) The apostle is speaking of struggles common to all people.

And this, I submit, is why the early Christians, who believed that Jesus was God's Son *in the flesh*, were also prompted to recall that Jesus, immediately after his baptism, spent some period in the desert, facing "the Tempter." In doing so, Jesus repeated the experience of ancient Israel and provided an example for his disciples. His temptations proved his humanity as an encouragement for those resolved to follow him.

Third, as though to further emphasize Jesus' humanity in this story, Mark mentions that during this time in the wilderness he was "with the wild beasts." That is to say, in his experience of temptation, Jesus returned to the situation of Adam, who lived with the animals.[2] Unlike Adam, however, he did not succumb to temptation.

Fourth, the period of forty days, during which Jesus was tempted, is a further correspondence to the "forty years" of Israel's time of testing in the wilderness. (I will presently mention the primitive catechetical significance of this allusion.)

Fifth, the tempter here in Mark is called "Satan," the demonic name derived from the book of Job. This is an important component in the story of Jesus' temptations. Consider the correspondence with Job: God has just identified Jesus as the Son "in whom *I am well pleased.*" Satan heard God say this about Jesus, just as he had heard of God's similar pleasure in Job:

> Have you considered My servant Job, that there is none like him
> on the earth, a blameless and upright man, one who fears God
> and shuns evil? (Job 1:8)

Satan, we recall, immediately challenged God on the point of Job's good standing, and he was given permission to smite the just man with grievous afflictions.

Here, likewise, right after Jesus' baptism—in which God expressed pleasure in His Son—Satan resolves to test the point: "Is God's pleasure in Jesus justified? Let's test it and see!" Satan, as we shall reflect presently, is "the Slanderer." He wants to give just men a bad reputation with the Almighty![3]

This parallel of Jesus with Job is of whole cloth with our consideration of Jesus' humanity because Job, too, was a standard type of the human situation. Like Adam, Job was subject to temptation.

Indeed, *man* is the very first word in the book named after Job, *'ish haya b'erets 'uts*—"A *man* there was, in the land of Uz" (Job 1:1, emphasis added). Job, the child of Adam, represents man's vulnerability in this world, where Satan is able to afflict him and put him to the test. In the story of Jesus' temptation, Satan appears once again to repeat that test. Jesus is not only the new Adam; he is also the new Job.

In sum, Mark's brief account of the temptations of Jesus discloses a considerable measure of Christian reflection on that event. For a more elaborate theological evaluation of it, we now turn to Matthew and Luke.

MORE COMPLEX STORIES

Whereas Mark tells the story of Jesus' temptations in just two verses, the other two gospel accounts of it are much longer: in Matthew eleven verses, in Luke thirteen verses.

Moreover, both Matthew and Luke describe three specific temptations by which Jesus was tried. Since the order of these temptations is not the same in both accounts, we will need to examine them separately at the point they diverge from each other.

They begin, however, very much the same way; I cite the wording in Matthew: "Then Jesus was led up by the Spirit into the wilderness to be tempted by the Slanderer [*ho Diabolos*]" (Matthew 4:1).

We should note how this opening differs slightly, first from Mark's version and second from Luke's.

First, whereas in Mark's story the tempter is called "Satan," Matthew and Luke (4:2) call him "the Slanderer" (*ho Diabolos*). This noun comes from the Greek (Septuagint) version book of Job, where the Slanderer is identical to Satan:

> Again there was a day when the sons of God came to present themselves before the Lord, and the Slanderer [*ho Diabolos*] came also among them to present himself. (Job 2:1 LXX)

Moreover, in both Matthew (4:10) and Luke (4:8), Jesus addresses the Slanderer as "Satan." The early church readily identified "Satan" and "the Slanderer" (*ho Diabolos*) with the ancient snake that first tempted Eve: "So the great dragon was cast out, that serpent of old, called the Slanderer and Satan, who deceives the whole world" (Revelation 12:9; cf. Mark 3:22–23).

Second, whereas Matthew says simply, "Jesus was led up by the Spirit," Luke expands the account to read,

Then Jesus, being *filled with the Holy Spirit*, returned from the Jordan and was led by the Spirit into the wilderness. (Luke 4:1, emphasis added)

In the portrayal of Jesus "filled with the Holy Spirit," we discern Luke's particular attention to this theme. The Spirit that led Jesus into the wilderness is the same Spirit that led old Simeon to the temple (Luke 2:27) and will, in due course, guide the missionary journeys of the apostles (Acts 8:29; 16:6–7). The description of Jesus as "filled with the Holy Spirit" repeats what Luke has already written of John the Baptist (1:15), Elizabeth (1:41), and Zacharias (1:67). He will also use this expression of those in the Upper Room on Pentecost (Acts 2:4), Simon Peter (4:8), the church at prayer (4:31), Stephen (6:3, 5; 7:55), Barnabas (11:24), and Paul (13:9).

TEMPTATION ONE—BREAD

Matthew and Luke agree that the first temptation in the wilderness was related to Jesus' hunger. Remarking that Luke's story is virtually identical, I cite Matthew:

> And when he had fasted forty days and forty nights, afterward he was hungry. Now when the Tempter [*ho Peirrazon*] came to him, he said, "*If* You are the Son of God, command that these stones become bread." (4:2–3, emphasis added)

The hypothesis—"if"—posed by the Tempter is based, of course, on the testimony of the voice from heaven, "This is My beloved Son." The Tempter is putting this very thesis to the test. *If* Jesus *is* God's Son, let him prove it! Turning stones to bread should be a pretty simple matter, after all, for God's Son.

Jesus, of course, will have none of this nonsense: "Man shall not live by bread alone," he responds, quoting Deuteronomy, "but by every word that proceeds from the mouth of God" (Matthew 4:4). Jesus' response solicits several comments.

First, the tempting demon is not permitted to dictate what is or is not appropriate to God's Son. The Slanderer knows nothing about it. Jesus does not argue the point with him. Eve, we recall, did argue with the demon (Genesis 3:1–5), and things did not go very well. For Jesus, this demon is not important; he is powerless, a nobody to be dismissed with a backhand brush from Deuteronomy.

Second, Jesus is no invulnerable, unthreatened superman. What authority (*exsousia*) and power (*dynamis*) he has as Son of God is for the benefit of other people, not himself. He will not "cash in" for personal advantage. We observe Jesus maintaining this rule throughout his ministry, to the very end:

Or do you think that I cannot now pray to my Father, and
He will provide me with more than twelve legions of angels?
(Matthew 26:53)

Third, Jesus uses Holy Scripture as a weapon against temptation. This rabbinic use of the Bible—as a weapon in the hour of trial—was taken up as an ascetical practice, which passed, in due course, to the Christian church and came to the special attention of the ancient Desert Fathers.

To this very day, the repetition of Bible verses, to be invoked in the hour of temptation, is called "sword drill," following the ancient persuasion that "the word of God is living and powerful, and sharper than any two-edged sword" (Hebrews 4:12). When believers seize hold of "the sword of the Spirit, which is the word of God" (Ephesians 6:17), they imitate the example of Jesus, who also invoked the book of Deuteronomy in the two subsequent temptations.

TEMPTATIONS TWO AND THREE

Matthew and Luke list differently the second and third temptations: Luke first speaks of a temptation on the mountain and then on the pinnacle of the temple; in Matthew these are reversed.

Although the original order of these stories is neither historically important nor theologically significant, the examination of the evidence does tell us something of the literary intention of each author. Perhaps, then, I may be granted a slight parenthesis to remark on this question:

Let us suppose that Luke's version represents the original order, with the temptation on the pinnacle of the temple coming last. If Luke's sequence was the original, why would Matthew change it?

There is good reason that Matthew may have changed it because the temptation on the mountain has the greater finality about it: "All these things I will give you if you will fall down and worship me" (Matthew 4:9). The magnitude of the demon's offense here, suggesting that Jesus submit to him, may have prompted Matthew to make this temptation final in the series.

This "final" temptation, which involves "all the kingdoms of the world" (Matthew 4:8), finds its parallel in the final chapter of Matthew, where, on "the mountain which Jesus had appointed for them," he commissioned them to "make disciples of all the nations" (Matthew 28:16–20). That is to say, if Matthew is the one responsible for putting the *mountain* temptation in the place of climax, it certainly fits well with the literary structure of his gospel.

But now, let us suppose that Matthew's sequence of the temptations was the original one. If Matthew's sequence was the original, why would Luke change the order so that the temptation at the temple comes as the climax of the story?

Actually, it is easy to see why this may have been the case because of the dominance of the temple in Luke's gospel. Luke both begins this work (Luke 1:9) and ends it (24:53) in the temple. Luke's infancy narrative culminates in the temple (2:46). Jerusalem, for Luke, is the place of finality. Only in Luke do we read that Jesus "steadfastly set His face to go to Jerusalem."[4] If Luke is the one responsible for putting the temple temptation in the place of climax, it certainly fits well with the literary structure of his gospel. In short, a good case can be made either way.

Whether in Matthew or Luke, therefore, let us look at the temptation on the pinnacle of the temple:

> Then the Slanderer [*ho Diabolos*] took him up into the holy city, set him on the pinnacle of the temple, and said to Him, "If You are the Son of God, throw yourself down. For it is written: 'He shall give His angels charge over you,' and 'In their hands they shall bear you up, / Lest you dash your foot against a stone.'" (Matthew 4:5–6; cf. Luke 4:9–11)

Once again, the test has to do with whether or not Jesus is the Son of God. If so, Jesus is invited to test the thesis himself. If he steps off the top of the temple, will God truly uphold him? The Tempter goes even further, proving that he, also, knows a thing or two about quoting Holy Scripture. To strengthen his temptation, he cites the promise in Psalm 91:11: "He shall give His angels charge over you."

Jesus' sonship, however, is not open to discussion. The Savior need not prove anything to anybody, certainly not to this arrogant demon. Jesus cites Deuteronomy again: "Jesus said to him, 'It is written again, "You shall not tempt the Lord your God"'" (Matthew 4:7; cf. Luke 4:12).

That is to say, Jesus is God's *obedient* Son. He will not force the Father's hand. He will assume to do nothing on his own. What he does is determined entirely by the Father's will, not his own. He always, and solely, be about the things of his Father.

Consequently, Jesus will not act rashly. That day will dawn—in due course and soon enough—when he *will* take the final leap. On that day, he will know, by experience, that God's angels will bear him up, lest he dash his foot on a stone. On that day, he will completely let go and allow himself to fall: "Father, into Your hands I commend my spirit" (Luke 23:46).

Third, and finally, in the temptation on the mountain the Tempter no longer even mentions the hypothetical "*If* you are the Son of God." This trial has to do, rather, with a direct challenge, which touches all authority (*exsousia*). In describing this temptation, Luke's wording is more ample:

> Then the Slanderer, taking him up on a high mountain, showed him all the kingdoms of the world in a moment of time. And the Slanderer said to him, "All this authority [*exsousia*] I will give you, and their glory; for it has been delivered to me, and I give it to whomever I wish. Therefore, if you will worship before me, all will be yours." (Luke 4:5–7; cf. Matthew 4:8–9)

The Tempter has moved a long way from Jesus' physical need for nourishment. Now the temptation is entirely spiritual. Jesus is presented with a demonic vision. In "a moment of time," he sees the world as Satan does. Satan offers him authority—*exsousia*—over all. In making this offer, the demon usurps the place of the Ancient of Days, who alone will give *exsousia* to the Son of Man (Daniel [in Greek] 7:13–14).

Jesus will obtain this *exsousia*, not from Satan, but from the Ancient of Days—through the experience of dying and rising again: *pasa exsousia edothe moi*, "all authority has been given to Me" (Matthew 28:18). This temptation represents Satan's invitation to avoid the cross. Once more citing Deuteronomy, Jesus spurns it:

Then Jesus said to him, "Away with you, Satan! For it is written, 'You shall worship the Lord your God, and Him only you shall serve.'" (Matthew 4:10; cf. Luke 4:8)

THE PASTORAL CONTEXT

Because each of these temptations seems to be dismissed so quickly, the reader will perhaps not pause to consider that they really *were* temptations. That is to say, Jesus really *was* hungry; Jesus really *did* feel the attraction of worldly power. He *was* tempted, insists the New Testament, "as we are" (Hebrews 4:15), and the gospel accounts of his experience were written down so that we might know that our high priest "can have compassion on those who are ignorant and going astray, since he himself is also subject to weakness" (Hebrews 5:2).

As observed earlier, Matthew and Luke describe Jesus' temptations in a way that contrasts his obedience in the desert with the disobedience of ancient Israel. Early Christian catechesis[5] regarded the time of Israel in the wilderness as of special significance, providing a pattern for the Christian experience in this world.[6]

Accordingly, the temptations of Jesus are told with an eye to Israel's desert experience. Both Matthew and Luke, in spite of differently arranging their narrative sequences, apparently relied on a common source, according to which the Savior quoted the book of Deuteronomy in response to each of the three temptations. This sustained appeal to the final book of the Torah—invoked as a weapon to resist temptation—summons the memory of Israel's moral failings during its forty years of desert wandering.

The immediate context of the two biblical accounts furthers this purpose: the parallel between Jesus' baptism and the passage through the Red Sea is followed immediately by the correspondence between the temptations of Jesus and Israel in the desert. (Mark also adheres to this sequence.)

For convenience, let us limit our attention to the Lukan narrative sequence:

Jesus meets the first temptation—"If you are the Son of God, command this stone to become bread"—by declaring, "Man shall not live by bread alone." This verse is lifted from the middle of Deuteronomy 8:1–6, which refers to ancient Israel's murmuring at the loss of their (alleged) better diet in Egypt (Exodus 16; Numbers 11).

Jesus answers the second temptation—the promise of world domination in exchange for fealty to Satan—by affirming, "You shall worship the Lord your God, and Him only you shall serve." This verse appears within Deuteronomy 6:10–15, in reference to Israel's repeated disposition to seek temporary advantage by worshipping alien gods (Exodus 23:23–33; Deuteronomy 12:30–31).

Jesus responds to the third temptation—"Throw yourself down from here"—by proclaiming, "You shall not tempt the Lord your God." This text, Deuteronomy 6:16, refers to Israel's constant disposition to tempt the Lord in the desert (cf. Exodus 17:1–7).

In all his temptations, then, the faithful response of Jesus is placed in direct contrast to Israel's infidelity during those forty sinful years of wandering. This was the "Bible lesson" that came directly out of early Christian catechesis.

AFTERMATH

Two final considerations are warranted with respect to Jesus' temptations:

First, the demons learned something from this experience. Through these temptations, the premise of the hypothesis "If You are God's Son" has now been established. Although the dark agencies are not really sure what this predication means, they do know it to be true.

Thus, when Jesus begins, very soon, to exorcize them from human souls, the demons have a clearer sense of what they are up against. In Mark's gospel, they are the first to "confess" it:

> Now there was a man in their synagogue with an unclean spirit. And he cried out, saying, "Let us alone! What have we to do with you, Jesus of Nazareth? Did you come to destroy us? I know who you are—the Holy One of God!" (Mark 1:23–24)

Since Jesus himself, however, was not yet prepared to proclaim his own identity in public, it was necessary for him to hush up these demons:

> Then he healed many who were sick with various diseases, and cast out many demons; and he did not allow the demons to speak, because they knew him. (Mark 1:34)

Second, Luke's account of Jesus' temptations ends with the hint that they will be renewed in due course: "Now when the Slanderer had ended every temptation, he departed from him *until an opportune time*" (Luke 4:13, emphasis added). This last expression, *achri kairou*, is not a merely chronological reference—"for a time." Luke has in mind, rather, a specific event (time as *kairos* or "instance," not *chronos*), a reference I suspect to mean Jesus' agony in the garden on the night before he died. As we shall observe when we come to it, that later scene portrays Jesus' supreme hour of trial.

5

THE PUBLIC MINISTRY

As WE BEGIN TO REFLECT ON THE PUBLIC MINISTRY OF Jesus, it is useful to observe that the four gospels neither follow an identical chronological sequence nor contain entirely the same material.

To many Bible readers—perhaps most—the gospel texts seem to indicate that Jesus' ministry lasted three years. This inference is based on two considerations:

First, John mentions three different observances of the Passover during Jesus' ministry: one just after the marriage at Cana (John 2:13), a second around the time of the multiplication of the loaves (6:4), and a third at the end of his life (11:55).

Second, Luke records a parable in which some readers find a paradigm of Jesus' ministry. This parable mentions three years:

A certain man had a fig tree planted in his vineyard, and he came seeking fruit on it and found none. Then he said to the keeper of his vineyard, "Look, for three years I have come seeking fruit on this fig tree and find none. Cut it down; why does it use up the ground?" But he answered and said to him, "Sir, let it alone this year also, until I dig around it and fertilize it. And if it bears fruit, well. But if not, after that you can cut it down."[1]

I comment on these two considerations in order:

First, John's first recorded Passover occurred *just after* the marriage at Cana. Hence, his chronological marks suggest that Jesus' ministry lasted just a bit over two years, not three years.

Second, the Lukan parable of the fig tree indicates that the examination lasts *four* years, not three: "for *three years* I have come seeking fruit" (plus) "let it alone *this year* also" (for a total of *four* years). If, therefore, the details of this parable are taken to represent the chronology of Jesus' ministry, then that ministry must have lasted four years. As far as I can determine, however, no one has seriously argued that Jesus' ministry lasted that long.

Consequently, I will stick with John's references to three celebrations of the Passover during the time of Jesus' ministry. Doing so, I conclude that that ministry lasted just a bit over two years.

Within that relatively short period, however, the chronology of the events themselves is less easy to determine. Modest and tentative estimates can be made. For example, because the multiplication of the loaves and Jesus' walking on water took place near the second Passover of his ministry (John 6:4) *and* Mark 6 records these same events, it may be legitimate to infer that other things recorded in Mark 6 also happened near the same time. These latter include Jesus' rejection at Nazareth and the missionary trip of the apostles (Mark 6:1–13). It may be inferred, in other words, that Jesus was rejected at Nazareth *and* sent out the missionary group about one year before his death.

No matter how reasonable that conclusion seems, nonetheless, the case is far from certain. As we shall reflect shortly, Mark's ordering of the events in Jesus' life was certainly determined—in the main—not by the restraints of historical chronology, but by a symmetric literary outline and the author's theological concerns. This is also true of the other Evangelists. Later in the present chapter, I will explain this phenomenon more carefully.[2]

By the time the four gospels were composed, it is safe to say that probably *nobody* was certain of the actual sequence of all the events in Jesus' life. It was not thought to be important. Other considerations, consequently, determined the order in which these stories were handed down in the church's catechesis (based on the apostles' preaching) and later recorded (in the four gospels).

Since, however, the earlier chapters of the present book have, on the whole, followed the narrative sequence found in Luke, it is probably useful, for the moment, to continue with Luke.

NAZARETH

Although Luke recognized that Jesus' public ministry did not actually begin at Nazareth (Luke 4:14–15, 23), he chose Jesus' arrival at that town as the point at which to dramatize its inauguration. Let us revisit, then, the scene at Nazareth, with which this book began:

> So he came to Nazareth, where he had been brought up. And as his custom was, he went into the synagogue on the Sabbath day, and stood up to read. And he was handed the scroll of the prophet Isaiah. And when he had opened the scroll, he found the place where it was written: "The Spirit of the Lord is upon me, / Because he has anointed me / To preach the gospel to the poor; / He has sent me to heal the brokenhearted, / To proclaim liberty to the captives / And recovery of sight to the blind, / To set at liberty those who are oppressed; / To proclaim the acceptable year of the Lord." Then he rolled up the scroll, and gave it back to the attendant and sat down. And the eyes of all who were in the synagogue were fixed on him. And he began to

say to them, "Today this Scripture is fulfilled in your hearing."
(Luke 4:16–21)

This is Luke's very solemn, detailed description of Jesus' first
sermon.[3] When the author wrote earlier, "Jesus increased in wisdom" (2:52), he not only stated a fact; he also initiated a line of
reflection, in the light of which to assess other facts—particular
events—in the life and ministry of Jesus: he grew and matured.
Luke, throughout his narrative, invites us to observe the Savior's
continuing growth in wisdom, and there is clear evidence of it here
in the event at Nazareth.

Up to this point in Jesus' public ministry, although we know
that "he taught in their synagogues" (Luke 4:15), there has been
no detailed description of his teaching. It is in the synagogue scene
at Nazareth that we find the full programmatic format of Jesus'
ministry: preaching the gospel, healing the blind, liberating those
in bondage, and relieving the various afflictions of the oppressed.
This Isaian text serves as a preview of what—in the course of Luke's
account—will soon come to pass.

Most striking about this appeal to Isaiah is the narrative
voice—the *who* is speaking. By declaring, "*Today* this Scripture is
fulfilled in *your* hearing," Jesus identifies himself as the real voice—
the "me"—of the Isaian text: "He has anointed *me*."

This identification of the speaker is given "from within": Jesus
recognizes *himself* as the voice speaking the words of the prophecy.
The inspired Scripture becomes the medium of Jesus' self-reflection.
He measures his ministry and calling—he knows God's will for
him—through his self-awareness expressed in the inspired words of
the prophet.

The key to this scene is conveyed in the opening line of the
Isaian text: "The Spirit of the Lord is *upon me* [*ep' eme*]." Luke, in
his description of the Savior's baptism, indicated how Jesus came to

know himself as the "me" in this prophecy: "And the Holy Spirit, in bodily form like a dove, came down *upon him [ep' avton]*." It was in the Holy Spirit's descent upon Jesus, we recall, that the Father addressed him as "you" and "Son": "*You* are My beloved *Son*; in *you* I am well pleased" (Luke 3:22, emphasis added).

When the Spirit descended on Jesus at his baptism, *something* changed. It was an event, with a before and after. Of course, Jesus already was conscious of himself as God's Son (cf. Luke 2:49), but this new experience at his baptism was decisive; it created, in his life, a then and *now*. He *grew*, he *increased*, through this experience; and, when he went through it, his family and friends recognized that *something* truly unique had happened to him. Indeed, they were disturbed by his new behavior.[4]

This personal experience of the Spirit's descent—to confirm the testimony of the Father's address—was integral to Jesus' increase in wisdom. By reason of that personal experience of the Father and the Holy Spirit, he recognized himself as the "me" in the Isaian prophecy—not as an objective fact but as a component of his subjective being. For this reason Jesus was able to proclaim that prophecy in the synagogue, not just as an ancient record, but as the divine message delivered to Israel in the here and now: "*Today* this Scripture is fulfilled in your hearing." In his proclamation, Jesus takes personal possession of the prophecy and assumes the full, immediate burden of its message. *He* is the bearer of God's word to Israel.

No one else in the world could read the prophecy as Jesus did, claiming complete and internal ownership of it. Luke implies that his hearers in the synagogue sensed the difference, inasmuch as "the eyes of all who were in the synagogue were fixed on him." This stunning description captures the full drama of the moment: Jesus' self-disclosure—the existential presentation of himself to Israel through the words of prophecy: "me," "today."

It seems important to consider the passage of time with respect to this event: during the interval separating the Lord's baptism and this later scene in the synagogue—a couple of months?—the reader senses Jesus' unseen growth in wisdom. Between the two events, the "wisdom" of the first event has "increased," to attain the further maturity revealed in the second.

During that interval, Luke informs us, "Jesus returned in the *power of the Spirit* to Galilee" (Luke 4:14, emphasis added). This reference to "the power of the Spirit" serves to connect these two dramatic Spirit-events in the maturing self-understanding of Jesus: his baptism and the reading of Isaiah at Nazareth.

SIGNS AND WONDERS

Although the Gospels testify that Jesus worked numerous miracles and performed all manner of healing, these stories never portray him as a wonder-worker of the sort we find among the biblical prophets, like Elijah and Elisha. If I were to use corresponding opposite adjectives to summarize the difference between Jesus and the biblical wonder-worker, the words that come to mind would be "easy" and "arduous." It all seems to come so easily to Christ, and he has an easy manner.

That is to say, those miracles that seem to take a certain measure of effort among the wonder-workers appear to be effortless in the case of Jesus. Elijah, for instance, prays for some time, and it starts to rain (1 Kings 18:41–45), whereas Jesus instantly stops a storm without a single syllable of prayer (Luke 8:22–25).

Or let us compare Elijah's raising of the widow's son to Jesus' raising of Jairus's daughter. In that earlier miracle, the prophet took the body, prayed over it, and enacted a ritual of petition for the child's revival (1 Kings 17:17–24). In the case of Jairus's little girl, on the other hand, Jesus made no petition: "He took the child by the hand, and said to her, '*Talitha, kum,*' which is translated, 'Darling, I say to you, arise'" (Mark 5:41).

The same is true in each of the other two cases where Jesus raised someone from the dead: Lazarus and the son of the widow of Nain. In each case, Jesus addressed the dead person with authority. Let us point out the obvious: there is more than a prophet here!

By way of introducing the subject of Jesus' miracles, let us restrict ourselves—for the moment, at least—to the seven "signs" around which John structures the first half of his own account of Jesus. A prevailing feature we note in nearly all of these signs is their sheer subtlety. We may regard them individually:

First, at Cana there is no discernible act by which the water is turned into wine. Jesus simply tells the servants to fill the water pots with water and then to take a cup of it to the steward of the wedding feast. That's it; nothing further. Nobody *sees* Jesus do anything. Yet, this was the occasion when "he *manifested* his glory; and his disciples believed in him" (John 2:11). The effect of the miracle was dramatic, but the doing of it completely escaped detection.

Not one whit less subtle is John's second sign, when the Savior tells the nobleman, "Go your way; your son lives." No one sees Jesus *do* anything; yet, a day later the nobleman learns, "*Yesterday* at the seventh hour the fever left him" (John 4:46–54). Like the preceding sign, this one involves no physical contact by Jesus.

But we do detect another common trait appearing in both signs; namely, obedience to a command: "*Fill* the water jars with water" (John 2:7) and "*Go* your way" (4:50). Disobedience to these commands, we presume, would mean no miracle!

Exactly the same traits—subtlety and obedience to command—characterize the third sign described by John, the healing of the paralytic at the pool of Bethesda:

Jesus said to him, "Rise, take up your bed and walk." And immediately the man was made well, took up his bed, and walked. (John 5:8–9)

Here, again, there is not the slightest indication how this happened. Jesus gave an order, the man obeyed it, and the thing was done.

We find these same qualities in the fourth sign, the multiplication of the bread and fish. First, there is a command: "Make the people sit down." Then, we are told,

Jesus took the loaves, and when he had given thanks he distributed them to the disciples, and the disciples to those sitting down; and likewise of the fish, as much as they wanted. (John 6:11)

A new element in the fourth sign is Jesus' handling of the food; it is multiplied as he gives it to those designated to distribute it to the crowd. The process of the actual increase, however, is no more perceptible than the agency that turned the water into wine. It happens "somewhere" between the giving hands of Jesus and the receiving hands of the people. The apostles, who "mediate" the event, are analogous to the servants who poured the water into the pots at Cana.

John's fifth sign—Jesus' walking on the water—may seem at first to stand by itself, inasmuch as it physically affected only Jesus. A closer inspection of it, however, shows that even this sign benefited the apostles. That is to say, after hours of struggling against a strong headwind, they immediately discovered that their "boat was at the land where they were going." Ironically, this story, also, has an expression of command, for Jesus tells the disciples, "Do not be afraid" (John 6:15–21).

The sixth sign in John's gospel likewise contains a command, when Jesus tells the man born blind, "Go, wash in the pool of Siloam" (John 9:7). There is subtlety here, as well: the miracle takes place outside of Jesus' physical presence.

The special feature in this sign has to do with the mud the man washed away from his eyes. John's description is graphic: "He spat on the ground and made clay with the saliva; and he anointed the eyes of the blind man with the clay" (John 9:6–7). Although Mark mentions two occasions when Jesus' spittle was the agent of healing (Mark 7:33; 8:23), the case of the blind man is, in this respect, unique to John. Still, the traits of subtlety and command are present in the story.

Jesus' final and culminating sign in the fourth gospel is the raising of Lazarus, a dramatic account told at length and in great detail. Although this miracle is emphatically *not* subtle, the component of command is still preserved. Indeed, it is doubled: "Take away the stone," *and* "Lazarus, come forth!" (John 11:39, 43).[5]

This final Johannine sign involves the voice of Jesus in a way not equaled in the previous six. It is Jesus' voice that causes the miracle of the dead man's rising. In fact, John had earlier foretold the power of Jesus' voice over the forces of death:

> Amen, amen, I say to you, the hour is coming, and now is, when the dead will hear the *voice* of the Son of God; and those who hear will live. . . . Do not marvel at this; for the hour is coming in which all who are in the graves will hear his *voice* and come forth. (John 5:25, 28–29, emphasis added)

Throughout the Gospels, Jesus often effects signs and wonders solely with the voice—"He cast out the spirits with a word" (Matthew 8:16)—but there is no uniform pattern in the immediate agency or means of these miracles, except, of course, that they come from Jesus.

Sometimes, it appears, Jesus simply exerts his inner will, as when the nobleman's son is healed. When he touches people to heal them, this is usually done with the hand. Apparently, however, it was not infrequent that "as many as had afflictions pressed about him to touch him" (Mark 3:10), without Jesus consciously doing anything. This is hardly surprising to those who believe that "in him dwells all the fullness of the Godhead bodily" (Colossians 2:9).

The divine power in Jesus' physical presence is clearest, I suppose, when John the Baptist, three months before his birth, reacted to that presence jubilantly. Elizabeth, John's mother, told the mother of Jesus, "As soon as the voice of your greeting sounded in my ears, the baby leaped in my womb for joy" (Luke 1:44). Jesus had this effect on people!

In most of the stories of his healings and exorcisms, however, there is a conscious, transpersonal encounter of the Savior with his beneficiaries. The stories of some of these encounters evidently passed into the apostolic preaching, where they were preserved and later written down in the Gospels.

Other such stories, however—especially in Luke—may have come, not from the apostolic preaching and general catechesis of the church, but from personal accounts communicated directly to the Evangelist. These would likely include the raising of the son of the widow (Luke 7:11–17), the restoration of the crippled woman in the synagogue (13:10–17), the cleansing of the ten lepers (17:11–19), and the encounter with Zacchaeus (19:1–10). That hypothesis explains why these events are peculiar to Luke's gospel and not contained in the others.

THE MOTHER-IN-LAW

When Jesus, in the first days of his ministry, made Capernaum a center of his ministry (Mark 1:21; Luke 4:23), he was closely associated with the home of Simon Peter. This early disciple, though he came from Bethsaida (John 1:44), had apparently moved a few miles westward to Capernaum, perhaps because of its fishing opportunities.

Jesus, centering his ministry at Capernaum, preached around a wide circuit (*kyklo*) that included Galilee and the coast towns of the

Sea of Galilee (Mark 6:6). He perhaps even lived at Peter's home. It was evidently here that he met his host's mother-in-law.

Mark's account is so lively and detailed that we suspect it represents an eyewitness account from Peter himself:[6]

> But Simon's wife's mother lay sick with a fever, and they told him about her at once. So he came and took her by the hand and lifted her up, and immediately the fever left her. And she served them. (Mark 1:30–31)

The parallel accounts of this scene in Matthew (8:14–15) and Luke (4:38–39) are much less vivid. Luke, for instance, omits the notice about Jesus "taking her by the hand."

An even more simplified version is given by Matthew, who mentions no one except Jesus and the ailing woman. According to this Evangelist, Jesus himself "sees" her lying feverish and acts on his own initiative. Then, at the end, the Evangelist says that the woman, when healed, "served *him*" rather than (as in Mark and Luke) "served them." Matthew thus transforms Peter's mother-in-law into the model believer, raised up by the Savior to be his servant.

THE CURIOUS CASE OF THE LEPER

The narrative sequence of the Synoptic Gospels places Jesus' healing of a leper very near the beginning of his ministry at Capernaum, shortly after the healing of Peter's mother-in-law.[7] In all three accounts, the leper approaches Jesus with the same abrupt request: "If you wanted to, you could cleanse me." After that, however, the story gets a bit more complicated.

In Mark's version—presumably the earliest of the three—the Savior's immediate response to the leper is . . . well, somewhat unexpected.

The original reading of the Markan passage, in my opinion, is that found in a fifth-century manuscript, the Codex Bezae: "Then Jesus, *becoming angry*, stretched out his hand and touched him, and said to him, 'I want to—Be cleansed!'" I am not aware, however, of any English translation that follows this reading in the Bezae manuscript.

Now, I admit that the Codex Bezae, in speaking of Jesus' *anger* in this scene, stands virtually alone among extant manuscripts of Mark. Nearly every other copy—including the oldest available to us—says that Jesus was "moved *with pity*" for the leper. Indeed, "pity" is exactly what we would expect here.

Why, then, do I prefer—perversely, perhaps—the manuscript that describes Jesus as "becoming angry" when he cleansed the leper?

In addressing this question, a first point to bear in mind is that this textual variation did not arise from confusion, inadvertence, or a scribal error. The variant reading is not the result of an accident. It is not possible that some ancient copyist, suffering from fatigue or distraction, accidentally substituted one word for another. In neither Greek nor English do these two expressions—"moved with pity" and "becoming angry"—even faintly resemble one another. Not even close. No, whoever altered the original wording of this verse did so deliberately.

Why, then, do I choose to trust a fifth-century manuscript (Codex Bezae), which says "becoming angry," over hundreds of other manuscripts that say "moved with pity"? How can I justify this preference?

I have already suggested the answer, I think: "Pity" is exactly the word we would expect here, not "anger." This expectation counts for something. It is easy to imagine any number of scribes—as they copied from an older manuscript—changing "becoming angry" to "moved with pity." On the other hand, it is virtually *impossible* to imagine a single scribe—of any period—deliberately changing "moved with pity" to "becoming angry."

Keeping in mind that the change—whoever made it—was deliberate, the change had to be made from "anger" to "pity," not the other way around. That is to say, it is inconceivable that anyone describing this scene would ascribe anger to Jesus unless there was reason to believe that Jesus was, in fact, angry. Anger is absolutely the last thing we would expect of Jesus when he cleansed the leper, so it is unthinkable that any Christian simply made it up!

On the other hand, it is not at all difficult to imagine that some scribe, copying from a manuscript that said "moved with anger"— and suspecting that the text in front of him was mistaken—decided to "correct" the text so that it would read "moved with pity." To any ancient scribe, "moved with pity" enjoyed the benefit of a prior likelihood because it is exactly what he expected to find at this point. And this is the very reason "pity" looks suspicious to me.

In fact, we know that many Christian scribes, over the centuries before the printing press, took it upon themselves to "correct" earlier biblical manuscripts when they thought those manuscripts to be mistaken.[8] The examples of this phenomenon are numerous. It should not surprise us, then, that Mark's reference to Jesus' "anger" in this scene may have shocked some Christian copyists, who presumed it was wrong.

Indeed, Mark's ready ascription of anger to Jesus was apparently a bit much even for the later gospels. Observe, for instance, how Luke (6:8) suppresses Mark's reference to the anger of Jesus in the story of the man with the withered hand (Mark 3:5). Luke (18:15–17) removes yet another reference of Mark to the indignation of Jesus (Mark 10:14).

Both Matthew and Luke, likewise, when they describe Jesus' cleansing of this leper, omit all mention of the Lord's emotions. It is hardly remarkable, then, that some early Christian scribes had trouble thinking of Jesus as angry when he cleansed the leper.

However, if we accept the manuscript (Codex Bezae) that says

Jesus became "angry," another problem remains. Having decided (as I have) that "becoming angry" is the correct description of Jesus as he cleansed the leper, I am obliged to explain that anger.

In this respect, I offer the following conjecture: on the other occasion when Mark describes Jesus as angry—the healing of the man with the withered hand—the reason given by the inspired writer is Jesus' perception of human heartlessness. Mark tells us Jesus "looked around at them with anger, being grieved by the hardness of their hearts" (Mark 3:5).

I suspect this is also the reason for Jesus' anger as he cleansed the leper: hardness of heart.

Jesus was surely not angry at the leper. It is not unreasonable, however, to think Jesus was angry at the social condition of this outcast (even though the Torah itself prescribed the physical separation of a leper). If we look more closely at the text, we discern that this leper's sense of personal worth was so reduced that he doubted, not that Jesus *could* cleanse him, but that Jesus would even *want to* cleanse him. Mark expresses this shunned man's misgiving by the hypothetical subjunctive—"if you wanted to" (*ean theleis*), a grammatical form hinting at the leper's deep personal apprehension on the point. He feared Jesus might *not* want to.

It is also significant that Jesus *touches* the poor untouchable here. By this extra gesture of intimate reassurance, he assumes the leper's uncleanness, as it were, the man's condition of ostracism. Henceforth, Mark observes, "Jesus could no longer openly enter the city, but was outside in deserted places." Jesus symbolically took the leper's place as an outcast.

NARRATIVE SEQUENCE

A close study of any one of the Gospels should dispel any notion that their authors were much interested in the chronology of Jesus' life—except to put Jesus' baptism first and his resurrection last. Otherwise, the narrative sequences in the Gospels seem to be dictated by other considerations, both literary and theological. The sacred writers had certain points they wanted to make, and they were not fussy about the exact order in which the events themselves actually happened.

For example, two parallel cycles of events give form to the narrative structure of Mark 6:30–8:30. The sequence of stories in each cycle is identical to the other, following an order of close symmetry that was certainly not accidental and can hardly be ignored. To wit:

1) Two Multiplications of the Loaves: Mark 6:30–44 and 8:1–9
2) Two Boat Trips: Mark 6:45–56 and 8:9–10
3) Two Disputes with Pharisees: Mark 7:1–13 and 8:11–13
4) Two Discourses on Bread: Mark 7:14–30 and 8:14–21
5) Two Miraculous Healings: Mark 7:31–37 and 8:22–26

This repeated narrative sequence is so obviously artificial that it defies any effort to regard it as chronologically probable. Without even looking at the other parts of Mark—for now—we recognize that he crafted and structured his story of Jesus as carefully as Homer did the *Iliad* or Dante *The Divine Comedy*. A careful comparison of the scenes in each element of Mark's double sequences reveals a great deal of his theology, but it tells us nothing at all about the chronology of Jesus' life.

I picked this example at random, because Mark is far from unique in this respect. It is fairly easy to go through each of the four gospels and discover how the narrative arrangements are based on literary considerations and theological premises—such as the five great discourses in Matthew, the journey motif in Luke, the "book of signs" in the first half of John. To mention these instances, moreover, is only to scratch the surface. The fabric of each gospel is closely woven with respect to structure, themes, and images; historical chronology has almost nothing to do with it.

There are small exceptions, of course, perhaps the most obvious being the narrative unity of the stories of Jairus's daughter and the woman with the issue of blood. In all three versions of this event,[9] the two miracles—which do not appear to be joined by a common theme and have almost no shared details[10]—are interwoven in a way difficult to explain, unless early Christian tradition actually remembered them as happening at the same time.

There *appears* to be a parallel case in the sequential ordering of the storm at sea and the Gadarene demoniac. In all three of the Synoptics,[11] these scenes are arranged in sequence. Furthermore, one can reasonably argue that this sequence represents a real historical memory, inasmuch as the drowning of the Gadarene pigs took place in Gentile territory (Jews not being permitted to tend pigs) on the east side of the Sea of Galilee, a place requiring a journey by boat. Thus, the sequence seems perfectly consistent with a distinct historical memory.

Well, perhaps, but let us not be too hasty on the point. Prior to examining this question, it may be good to reflect on another aspect of the gospel tradition—the transition from preaching to writing. These two stories may help us grasp this process.

A STORM, SOME DEMONS, AND QUITE A FEW PIGS

Although the Gospels are placed in the New Testament *in front of* the Epistles, the actual historical order of the works was entirely reversed. That is to say, when Paul wrote his letters between roughly AD 49 and 63, not a single one of the Gospels had been composed. In comparison with the rest of the New Testament, the Gospels were the "late" books. We have fairly firm historical testimony that the earliest of the Gospels, Mark, was not composed until after the fire at Rome in the summer of AD 64.

The relative "lateness" of the Gospels hardly means, of course, that their narrative material was unknown to the early Christians. No one will seriously contend that between AD 33 (or so) and 65 nobody knew what Jesus did and taught!

In fact, behind each of the Gospels was a vast amount of Christian preaching and catechesis. Very little was written down in the Gospels that had not been preached and taught. For instance, from earliest times we have widespread testimony that Mark's gospel was based on his immediate and firsthand memory of Peter's preaching in Rome.[12]

Now, one thing preachers do is arrange their material according to preferred and chosen themes.[13] Only rarely, and by accident, has a preacher been much concerned with points of chronology. Consequently, if the gospel stories were preserved in patterns determined by preaching and reinforced by decades of the same, we should expect the gospel sequences to be thematic, not chronological. And this is, in fact, what we find.

Let me suggest we may have an instance of this phenomenon in the stories of the storm at sea and the drowning of all those pigs. Let us look more carefully at these two stories.

First, there was the storm:

> On the same day [after the seed parables], when evening had come, he said to them, "Let us cross over to the other side." Now when they had left the multitude, they took him along in the boat as he was. And other little boats were also with him. And a great windstorm arose, and the waves beat into the boat, so that it was already filling. But he was in the stern, asleep on a pillow. And they awoke him and said to him, "Teacher, do You not care that we are perishing?" (Mark 4:35–38)

The reader is struck by the vividness of Mark's account. He had commenced his gospel, we recall, by announcing the "beginning of the gospel of Jesus Christ, the *Son of God*" (Mark 1:1, emphasis added), but here he goes into some detail to portray the *humanity* of Jesus, sound asleep in the midst of a storm.

Recalling the ancient tradition that Mark's material came from Peter, we observe the graphic details indicating that this story represents firsthand testimony: the churning water, the dangerous wind, the peril of the little boat, and the growing anxiety of the crew.[14]

They cried out. Indeed, they had a proper model in the words of the psalmist, who declared,

[God] commands and raises the stormy wind,
Which lifts up the waves of the sea.
They mount up to the heavens,
They go down again to the depths;
Their soul melts because of trouble.
They reel to and fro, and stagger like a drunken man,
And are at their wits' end.
Then they cry out to the Lord in their trouble.
    (Psalm 107:25–28)

The response of Jesus was immediate:

Then he arose and rebuked the wind, and said to the sea, "Peace, be still!" And the wind ceased and there was a great calm. But he said to them, "Why are you so fearful? How is it that you have no faith?" And they feared exceedingly, and said to one another, "Who can this be, that even the wind and the sea obey him!" (Mark 4:39–41)

Who can this be? Mark's readers know exactly who this is because Mark identified him from the start: "the beginning of the gospel of Jesus Christ, *the Son of God.*"

Up to this point in Mark's account, however, only the demons have been able—in some measure—to answer the question, "Who can this be?" (Mark 1:32–34). For now, the apostles' question remains unanswered.

It will be answered, nonetheless, in the story that immediately follows—the account of the demons and the pigs:

> Then they came to the other side of the sea, to the country of the Gadarenes. And when he had come out of the boat, immediately there met him out of the tombs a man with an unclean spirit, who had his dwelling among the tombs; and no one could bind him, not even with chains, because he had often been bound with shackles and chains. And the chains had been pulled apart by him, and the shackles broken in pieces; neither could anyone tame him. And always, night and day, he was in the mountains and in the tombs, crying out and cutting himself with stones. When he saw Jesus from afar, he ran and fell down before him. And he cried out with a loud voice and said, "What have I to do with You, Jesus, *Son of the Most High God?*" (Mark 5:1–7, emphasis added)

Here, then, we find the correct answer to the question posed at the end of the previous scene: "Who can this be?" Answer: "Jesus, Son of the Most High God." This combination of query and response, found in sequence in all three Synoptics, suggests that the demons themselves are answering the question that the apostles have just asked.

This is curious. The question, "Who is Jesus?" was, in fact, a basic pre-baptismal question. Recall the story of Philip and the Ethiopian, who said to him,

"See, here is water. What hinders me from being baptized?" Then Philip said, "*If you believe* with all your heart, you may." And he answered and said, "I believe that *Jesus Christ is the Son of God.*" (Acts 8:36–37, emphasis added)

The question asked in the storm scene, therefore, represents the fundamental inquiry that brings individuals to faith in Jesus: "Who do *you* say that I am?" Here in the two sequential gospel scenes—the storm and the demoniac—we find that fundamental question stated and answered. It was a baptismal question.

It is hardly surprising, therefore, that this question is answered *at the waterside*, the place immediately beside the baptismal waters. In Mark (especially), the waterside is a common site where potential believers encounter Jesus: the first disciples (Mark 1:16–19), Levi (2:13–14), the great crowds (3:7–9), the sick (6:53–55), the deaf mute (7:31–32), and the blind man (8:22). This suggestion of conversion and repentance at the waterside evokes the imagery of baptism.

This poor demoniac, then, represents Mark's second storm scene, as it were, a terrible turmoil of the soul corresponding to the squall on the lake. The man's situation is desperate and dire. Jesus asks him, "What is your name?" And he answers, "My name is Legion; for we are many." Now, a Roman legion had six thousand infantry. This demoniac is, in short, a totally possessed fellow. No matter. Jesus dispatches these six thousand demons into two thousand pigs. Three demons, that is, per pig.

At the end of the storm on the lake we were informed, "The wind ceased and there was a great calm" (Mark 4:39). So, too, in this corresponding second scene:

Then they came to Jesus, and saw the demon-possessed man, who had the legion, sitting and clothed and in his right mind. (Mark 5:15)

Does the juxtaposition of these two scenes—the storm and the demoniac—represent a preaching motif of early Christian preaching, a remnant of pre-baptismal catechesis, or does it simply mean the two events actually followed each other in sequence? It is difficult to say, but it is also unnecessary to decide. The two stories clearly belong together, which is doubtless the reason all three Synoptics put them together. Christian readers have long read them together, and Christian preachers have, with marvelous frequency, made them components in the same sermon.

6

LEARNING AND TEACHING

AMONG THE LIMITATIONS CONSEQUENT TO THE INCARNATION, it is important to consider whether they included the eternal Word's assumption of human *ignorance*. This, too, would seem to be part of the "human condition," after all.

When Luke tells us, "Jesus increased in wisdom" (Luke 2:52), the plain meaning of the statement implies that he progressed from less wise to wiser. He necessarily began with less wise, and from that he "increased."

Now, an "increase" implies the making up of a deficiency, the overcoming of a limitation. Logically prior to learning certain things, Jesus was *ignorant* of them. In short, the limits of the Incarnation included Jesus' experience of ignorance.

In fact, there appear to be signs of this in the Gospels. Thus, when the disciples petitioned Jesus for some sort of timetable for the end of the world, he answered, "But of that day and hour no one knows, not even the angels in heaven, nor the Son, but only the Father" (Mark 13:32; cf. Matthew 24:36). Even referring to himself as God's Son, Jesus confessed he had no information about the "day and hour" of his own coming at the end of time. Did Jesus mean this, or was he indulging some sort of mental gymnastics?

79

Similarly, if Jesus already knew the name of the Gadarene demon, why did he ask, "What is your name?" (Luke 8:30). It is difficult to imagine the Savior was just trying to be chatty with the demon.

Likewise, should we imagine that Jesus was "faking it," *pretending* not to know the answer, when he asked Mary and Martha about the dead Lazarus, "Where have you laid him?" (John 11:34). Unless we suppose that Jesus did not know where Lazarus was buried, it is nearly impossible to think of another reason he might have made inquiry on the point.

This is a curious consideration because, just days earlier, Jesus already *knew* Lazarus was dead, even though no one had told him (John 11:11–14). So . . . Jesus *knew* Lazarus was dead, but he did not know where he was buried. What does this mean?

Some Christians find it uncomfortable to think of ignorance as part of Jesus' experience. They imagine—and occasionally insist—that the Savior's subjective knowledge included access to the divine omniscience: He knew everything! Indeed, they point out, didn't Simon Peter actually tell Jesus, "Lord, you *know all things*; you know that I love you" (John 21:17)? And doesn't that settle it?

Not actually. If the traditional Christian interpretation of Jesus (that defined by the ancient councils and enshrined in the ancient creeds) is correct, there is no reason to suppose that the human mind of Jesus enjoyed access to the divine omniscience, and there is no evidence in the Gospels that that was the case.

On the contrary, if we accept the plain meaning of the biblical material, we are obliged to infer that Jesus did *not* know everything.[1] The opposite supposition would mean that the eternal Word was not completely enfleshed. It would imply that God's Son was not *fully* incarnate. He was holding something back. He did not quite "empty himself." When, being rich, for our sake he became poor, he palmed a coin or two, as it were. In short, he did not assume a fully human existence.

This notion, however, is not what we find in either the Gospels or the defined Christology of the Christian church.

What, then, about the questions Jesus asked? I want to argue that those questions did not always imply ignorance on his part.

On a few occasions, of course, it is difficult to be sure of the intent of Jesus' questions. For instance, when the sick woman in the crowd put out her hand and touched the hem of his robe, Jesus inquired, "Who touched me?" (Luke 8:45). While it is perfectly reasonable to think that Jesus did not know who touched him (and this is how the apostle Peter understood the question), it is by no means unlikely that Jesus had something quite different in mind— namely, to invite this anonymous woman to come forward and be recognized. (I will deal with this scene later in the book.)

Also, take the instance when Jesus asked, "Nevertheless, when the Son of Man comes, will he really find faith on the earth?" (Luke 18:8). It is not obvious to me that this was a rhetorical question. The context suggests, rather, that the question had a real answer, and Jesus was not entirely certain of that answer. Observe that his "nevertheless" puts the query in opposition to his previous assertion that God will speedily avenge his elect (18:7–8). That is to say, Jesus, even as he was sure that God would avenge the righteous, seemed to be wondering if there would be any righteous left to avenge. I think a certain distress can be discerned in his voice at this point.

Likewise, when Jesus asked the apostles, "When I sent you without money bag, knapsack, and sandals, did you lack anything?" (Luke 22:35), did he already know the answer? Perhaps, but not, I think, necessarily.

PROPHETIC DISCERNMENT

This subject needs to be handled carefully and, I believe, under the guidance of two chief considerations, both of which encourage circumspection:

First, it is a fact that in the Gospels Jesus manifests an extraordinary spiritual perception, a familiarity with matters far beyond the normal human ken. For instance, when he instructs the disciples to prepare for the final Passover meal, Jesus tells them,

> Behold, when you have entered the city, a man will meet you carrying a pitcher of water; follow him into the house that he enters. (Luke 22:10)

Here the Savior knows, ahead of time, that the disciples, when they enter Jerusalem, will run into a man carrying a pitcher of water. This will be a special sign to them because men in the Holy Land never carried water. (It was a woman's task. This custom, by the way, has not changed much in the Middle East.)

How, then, did Jesus know about this man who would be carrying water somewhere near the city gate? More than one explanation is possible. For instance, this assigned token may have been arranged earlier, by an agreement between Jesus and the man in question. Since the gospel story does not seem to treat the event as miraculous, this is a perfectly rational explanation of the thing.

I suspect this to be the wrong explanation, however. In this particular instance, I am more disposed to interpret Jesus' foreknowledge of the event as an example of prophetic insight. This phenomenon is not uncommon among the biblical prophets. Examples abound.

Consider for a moment the case of Ahijah, whose prophetic ministry is recorded in 1 Kings. It was Ahijah, we recall, who prophesied to Jeroboam the schism of the Davidic kingdom after the death of Solomon (1 Kings 11:29–39). That prediction, based on prophetic insight, was justified in the event. We do not again hear of Ahijah for a long time, nor does the Bible give us reason to suppose that the prophet was ever again approached for advice in the governance of the realm.

Years later, nonetheless, Jeroboam does feel the need to consult Ahijah, who has now grown very old and dim of eye. The king's son is sick, so Jeroboam dispatches his wife to the prophet in hopes of obtaining a favorable word from God. Jeroboam sends her, moreover, in disguise, evidently too embarrassed to let Ahijah know who it is that seeks his word. Even before the queen enters the room, nonetheless, Ahijah knows who she is and what she wants. He had been able to read the signs of the times during the reign of Solomon; this gift of clairvoyance has not left him. Inwardly guided by the Almighty, Ahijah discerns the situation perfectly, and the Lord himself dictates "thus and thus" what he is to say (1 Kings 14).

There is no suggestion, obviously, that Ahijah had access to the divine omniscience. What he knew was revealed to him through the insight of revelatory prophecy. The Old Testament is full of such examples—Samuel, Elijah, Elisha, and others—nor can I think of any reason why Jesus would have been less gifted, in this respect, than the prophets.

When, therefore, we find Jesus knowing things beyond the normal human ken, it is useful to remember that his contemporaries also noticed this about him. Moreover, their recognition of this phenomenon prompted them to liken him to the prophets. The prophets, they knew, could read hearts and discern the signs of the times. When his contemporaries perceived this heightened spiritual awareness in Jesus, therefore, they spontaneously thought of him as a prophet.

We may take the example of Jesus with the Samaritan woman at the well (a story we will examine later on at some length). At one point in their conversation, we recall, after Jesus told the woman, "Go, call your husband," she replied—with some measure of embarrassment—"I have no husband." Then, to her amazement, Jesus answered, "You have well said, 'I have no husband,' for you have had five husbands, and the one whom you now have is not your husband; in that you spoke truly" (John 4:16–18).

With respect to our subject here, what is most striking in this story is the woman's reaction to this statement: "Sir, I perceive that you are a *prophet*" (4:19). She recognized that Jesus manifested a mark of a prophet: He knew and could speak about secret and hidden matters, things he could not, in normal circumstances, be expected to know. This Jesus, she announced to her compatriots, "told me all that I ever did" (4:39). The Samaritan woman, confronted with this level of spiritual insight, promptly pegged him a prophet.

In short, there is not sufficient evidence in the gospel stories that the mind of Jesus had access to the divine omniscience, and traditional Christology prompts us not to ascribe it to him. Thus, if Jesus knew the appointed man would be carrying a pitcher of water and knew the secret details of the life of this Samaritan woman, he surely knew the sorts of things a prophet might be expected to know.

And this, I submit, is how we should regard the case of Lazarus's tomb. Jesus knew exactly two things about that situation in Bethany because he only needed to know two things—namely, "Lazarus is dead" and "I go that I may wake him up" (John 11:11–14). This level of insight—to say nothing of this level of assurance—was quite compatible with Jesus' not knowing where Lazarus was buried.

Holy Scripture provides a parallel example in a story of Saul and Samuel: Even before he meets Saul, Samuel receives a prophetic revelation of who he is and what he is doing. He reveals this to Saul—along with quite a bit more—when he first meets him (1 Samuel 9:15–10:8). By prophetic discernment, Samuel knows certain things about Saul, but there is no evidence that he knows *everything*.

Perhaps more challenging, with respect to this subject, are those occasions when we find Jesus reading men's thoughts. Let us consider an instance of this phenomenon that Mark placed very early in his narrative:

And some of the scribes were sitting there and reasoning in their hearts, "Why does this Man speak blasphemies like this? Who can forgive sins but God alone?" But immediately, when Jesus perceived in his spirit that they reasoned thus within themselves, he said to them, "Why do you reason about these things in your hearts?" (Mark 2:6–8)

Especially with regard to the hearts of his enemies, the Gospels tell us, "Jesus knew their thoughts,"[2] and "Jesus perceived their wickedness" (Matthew 22:18).

Once again, however, Jesus' capacity to discern the inner thoughts of others seems to be a mark, not of divine omniscience, but of an unusually perceptive spiritual sensitivity. Doubtless, we should ascribe his extraordinary gift of spiritual discernment to the influence and guidance of the Holy Spirit.

In one recorded case, this spiritual sensitivity of Jesus seems so extraordinary that no obvious comparison among the Old Testament prophets comes readily to mind. This is the scene when Jesus meets Nathaniel for the first time. It is useful to cite the passage at length:

Jesus saw Nathanael coming toward Him, and said of him, "Behold, an Israelite indeed, in whom is no deceit!" Nathanael said to Him, "How do You know me?" Jesus answered and said to him, "Before Philip called you, when you were under the fig tree, I saw you." Nathanael answered and said to Him, "Rabbi, You are the Son of God! You are the King of Israel!" (John 1:47–49)

Since the inspired writer does not relate—much less explain— the earlier experience to which this dialogue refers, the reader is disposed to tread lightly. This story does, however, seem to indicate that Jesus declared himself to have been a witness ("I saw you") to some prior spiritual "event" Nathaniel had experienced. Jesus even identified the physical setting of that experience: "under the fig tree." Apparently shocked and deeply moved by this revelation, Nathaniel makes what appears to be the first full creedal profession of Christology recorded in the New Testament: "You are the Son of God!"

With regard to that experience, I suspect the closest biblical parallel may be the experience of Ananias of Damascus, to whom God revealed the inner conversion experience of the apostle Paul, even as Paul was made (internally) aware of the coming visit of Ananias (Acts 9:10–16).

The traditional Christology of the Christian church holds that in Jesus there was only one person, a single center of subjectivity. That is to say, Jesus did not sometimes think as human and sometimes as divine. Everything he knew, he knew through human experience, no matter how refined, elevated, and unique. All his "thinking" took place in a human brain at the service of a *human* intellect because Jesus was (and is) God's Son enfleshed in a human condition.[3]

QUESTIONS AND CONFRONTATIONS

Second, although Jesus asked questions, most often—it appears— he did not ask questions in order to obtain information. In fact, he employed questions in a variety of ways.

Sometimes he asked purely rhetorical questions.[4] He occasionally used ironic, subtle, and sarcastic questions to confound and reprove his adversaries.[5] On other occasions, when his enemies attempted to confound him by an interrogation, Jesus met them with yet another question. This practice was the traditional rabbinical counterquestion. We see him do this when questioned about the Sabbath (Matthew 12:10–12), about fasting (15:1–3), about paying taxes to Caesar (22:15–20), and about his own authority (21:23–25).

When Jesus asked a sequence of hypothetical questions—"if" and "unless"—the effect could convey an elementary lesson in logic:

> *If* Satan casts out Satan, he is divided against himself. How then will his kingdom stand? And *if* I cast out demons by Beelzebub, by whom do your sons cast them out? . . . Or how can one enter a strong man's house and plunder his goods, *unless* he first binds the strong man? (Matthew 12:26–29, emphasis added)

A question is just as likely to *convey* truth as to *seek* it. If asking questions is a good way of learning, it is an even better way of teaching. Good teachers ask questions. Consequently, Jesus chiefly employs the interrogatory form as a mode of teaching. Jesus asks questions, moreover, just about as much as he tells parables. For this reason, we need to consider Jesus more closely as the Teacher, the *Rabbi.*

The Semitic expression "Rabbi" appears to have been a title most readily applied to Jesus during his public ministry.[6] This usage is best preserved in John's gospel, where "Rabbi" (or "Rabbouni," *my* Rabbi) is a standard way for people to address Jesus.[7] The word essentially means "Teacher."

The first time John wrote "Rabbi," however, he made a point of translating it into Greek—*didaskalos*—perhaps because not all his readers were familiar with the Semitic term. This was the early occasion when

> two disciples heard [John the Baptist] speak, and they followed Jesus. Then Jesus turned, and seeing them following, said to them, "What do you seek?" They said to him, "*Rabbi*" (which is to say, when translated, *Teacher*), "where are you staying?" (John 1:37–38, emphasis added)

The equivalence of *Rabbi* and *Didaskalos* was also indicated in the first words Nicodemus spoke to Jesus: "*Rabbi*, we know that you are a *didaskalos* come from God" (John 3:2). John also provides the Greek translation of "Teacher" when Mary Magdalene calls Jesus "Rabbouni" (cf. John 20:16). Often enough, as well, John simply sticks with the Greek *didaskalos*, instead of the Semitic word.[8]

Mark, who goes the furthest in maintaining original Semitic expressions in his story of Jesus,[9] also preserves "Rabbi" or "Rabbouni" as a title by which the disciples addressed Jesus.[10] More often, however, Mark simply gives the Greek word,[11] especially in the case of direct address.[12]

In Luke[13] and—on the whole—in Matthew,[14] the Greek word for "Teacher" replaces the Semitic "Rabbi." Thus, in one form or another—and constantly by implication—the first disciples thought of Jesus chiefly as "Teacher."

As mentioned earlier, controlled and directed questioning is an effective form of teaching because questions actively engage the students' mental processes. When lectured, the person takes in what the teacher says, but when questioned, the same person is invited to formulate a thought, to engage the lesson in the active processes of his own mind.

A competent teacher frequently solicits responses that accomplish this. He will ask such questions as: "Who is a faithful and wise servant, whom his master made ruler over his household, to give them food in due season?"[15]

PEDAGOGY

A pedagogical question could cover a variety of cases:

Like any teacher, for example, Jesus asked questions to which he already knew the answers or to which the answers were inconsequential or the answers were presupposed, or the questions themselves simply required no response. For instance, "Can the friends of the bridegroom mourn as long as the bridegroom is with them?" (Matthew 9:15). And, "which is greater, the gold or the temple that sanctifies the gold?" (23:17).

Often enough, the answers are implied in the wording of the question: "Do you suppose that I came to give peace on earth?" (Luke 12:51).

Sometimes Jesus' questions served to solicit faith.[16] On occasion a question could embody—or replace—a reprimand.[17] Jesus used questions, likewise, to introduce similes, parables, or metaphors. In these cases, the function of the question was mainly to supply rhetorical elaboration, to provide a moment of reflective pause, to facilitate reflection.[18]

Now and then Jesus asked a question *because* he knew the answer. Thus, we are told, "When Jesus perceived their thoughts, he answered and said to them, 'Why are you reasoning in your hearts?'" (Luke 5:22). Here we have an instance of a spiritual perception leading to an explicit query. Jesus surely did not expect an answer to this question; he asked it, rather, in order to put his enemies on notice that he "had their number"—and knew it to be low.

On occasion, Jesus asked questions precisely *in order to* answer them:

> "Who is my mother and who are my brothers?" And he stretched
> out his hand toward his disciples and said, "Here are my mother
> and my brothers!" (Matthew 12:48–49)

When the situations called for it, Jesus used interrogation to put people on the spot and oblige them to think twice. For example, "Have you come out, as against a robber, with swords and clubs?" (Luke 22:52). And, "What man of you, having a hundred sheep, if he loses one of them, does not leave the ninety-nine in the wilderness, and go after the one which is lost until he finds it?" (Luke 15:4).

From time to time, Jesus' questions encouraged the listener to make calculations, to gauge estimates, to line up comparisons for assessment. Questions of this sort could be expressed in almost syllogistic form, suggesting, for example, the relation between premise and inference—"if" and "what"—as though the listener were computing a market projection:

> If you love those who love you, *what credit* is that to you? . . . And
> *if* you do good to those who do good to you, *what credit* is that to
> you? . . . And *if* you lend to those from whom you hope to receive
> back, *what credit* is that to you? (Luke 6:32–34, emphasis added)[19]

With respect to the logic of premise and inference, let us recall that Jesus "did business." He worked for a living, supporting himself and his mother. Laboring with his hands, he dealt with clients and customers. As a craftsman with certain skills to barter, he thought of life in terms of profit and loss, of gain and exchange. So we feel no surprise at his inquiring,

> What does it *profit* a man if he *gains* the whole world, and *loses*
> his own soul? Or what will a man give in *exchange* for his soul?
> (Matthew 16:26, emphasis added)

When Jesus asked, "What do you think?" he mainly had in mind to *make* people think.[20] As efforts of calculation, questions also served as a summons to plain and simple rationality. Jesus sometimes felt obliged to point out the obvious: "Can the blind lead the blind? Will they not both fall into the ditch?" (Luke 6:39). Or, "Salt is good; but if the salt has lost its flavor, how shall it be seasoned?" (14:34).

A series of questions could serve to drive home a single point:

What did you go out into the wilderness to see? A reed shaken
by the wind? But *what* did you go out to see? A man clothed in
soft garments? . . . But *what* did you go out to see? A prophet?
(Matthew 11:7–9, emphasis added)

Following the same pattern, an interrogative series could serve
as a review of past lessons:

"Do you not yet understand, or remember the five loaves of
the five thousand and how many baskets you took up? Nor the
seven loaves of the four thousand and how many large baskets
you took up?" (Matthew 16:9–10)

Like all good pedagogues, Jesus asked questions to make sure
the disciples were able to follow what he was telling them: "Have
you understood all these things?" (Matthew 13:51). Or, more insis-
tently, "Are you also still without understanding?" (15:16).

Especially on the point of discipleship, Jesus' questions were
sometimes out-and-out challenges. "Do you also want to leave?" he
asked the apostles (John 6:67). And of James and John he inquired,
"Are you able to drink the cup that I drink, and be baptized with the
baptism that I am baptized with?" (Mark 10:38).

INVITATIONS

On occasion, questions from Jesus served the purpose of engaging
the disciples in either a discussion or an activity, making them participants in an event. Recall how he engaged Philip at the time of the
multiplication of the loaves:

> Jesus lifted up his eyes, and seeing a great multitude coming toward him, he said to Philip, "Where shall we buy bread, that these may eat?" But this he said to test him, for he himself knew what he would do. (John 6:5–6)

What, then, was accomplished by this question to Philip, since Jesus already "knew what he would do"? His question here served the purpose of evoking the assistance of the apostles in what was about to take place.

Jesus did not ask that question for Philip's sake, I believe, but for Andrew's. They were a pair. He knew that wherever you saw Philip, Andrew must be nearby.[21] The question was apparently meant to be overheard by Andrew, who promptly replied, "There is a lad here who has five barley buns and a couple of dried fish" (John 6:9). *Now* they could get started!

Thus, by putting to Philip a question to which he already knew the answer, Jesus transformed these apostles from mere spectators to active participants in the experience of the multiplication of the loaves. It is *they* who will seat the people for the meal (John 6:10). It is *they* who will distribute the bread and fish (6:11). In this scene, then, Jesus' question both commences the event and provides for its participatory structure.

Something similar was at play, it seems, when Jesus asked the blind man at Jericho, "What do you want Me to do for you?" Jesus knew the man was blind, so why did he ask the question? Well, it served as an invitation for the blind man (Bartimaeus, Mark tells us) to ask—to engage Jesus in a give-and-take. It elevated the dignity of the blind man. It engaged him as an active person. The question was a summons, a bidding, an invitation to express and take possession of his faith in Jesus. And, in fact, this is exactly what happened:

He said, "Lord, that I may receive my sight." Then Jesus said to him, "Receive your sight; your faith has made you well." (Luke 18:41–42)

It is no wonder that Mark finishes this story by remarking of the blind man, "And immediately he received his sight and *followed Jesus* on the road" (Mark 10:52, emphasis added).[22]

Finally, when Jesus asked questions, he was sometimes *feigning ignorance!* It is not clear how often he did this during his earthly ministry, but once the cross was behind him—once he had completely conquered sin and death—Jesus seemed to relish this form of question almost—if I dare suggest it—as a form of entertainment! We will examine this delightful rhetorical device in the chapter on the Resurrection.

7

JESUS AT PRAYER

NO CONSIDERATION OF THE SAVIOR'S HUMANITY IS ADE-
quate, I believe, that fails to consider a simple fact mentioned
often in the Gospels: he prayed. Indeed, if we reflect that prayer
is the highest human activity—the defining purpose of human
existence and the goal of human destiny—we should say that
Jesus' prayer reveals more about him as a human being than anything else he did.

Before speaking of Jesus' prayer, let me offer a remark or two on
prayer as a human act. Even if done alone, prayer is not an exercise
of isolation. In prayer a human being is engaged with existence in
its fullness.

First, when a person prays, he represents the whole created
order, of which he is the conscious, self-reflective part. It is in the
prayer of human beings that creation becomes conscious of its relationship to God. Man is the *thinking* part of the cosmos. In the
entire material world, the only being that even thinks to pray is man.
Human thought is the only place where the cosmos is self-reflective.

Second, when someone prays, he represents history, which
has bequeathed to him the very language he uses to speak and to

think. To pray is to take an heir's possession—by language—of all that has transpired during man's existence in this world. We are no more able to separate ourselves from the time of human history than from the space of the created order. This is the reason, I believe, why the central day of Creation, the "fourth day"—Wednesday—provides the cosmic chronometer to measure man's time on the earth.[1]

Third, when someone prays, he renders active the highest potential present in every human heart. For this reason, the one who prays—the *orans* with upraised hand—represents the whole of human society, to which he is tied by a complex network of associations. Whether he reflects on it or not, no one ever prays except as the representative of his brothers and sisters.

To speak of the prayer of Jesus, therefore, requires a certain attention to other subjects, which include his conscious relationship to the created order, his perception of historical destiny (the vital role of Israel in history and the fulfillment of biblical prophecy), his social communion with his friends (the disciples, including ourselves), and—uniquely—his awareness of being God's only Son, the Father's final and defining revelation to the human race.

Let us start, then, with Jesus and the created order of time, space, and the social complexities that fill them.

PERSONAL PREFERENCE

Holy Scripture conveys the impression the Savior was fond of praying alone and out of doors. For instance, Mark writes of the earliest days of his ministry:

> Now in the morning, having risen a long while before daylight,
> he went out and departed to a solitary place; and there he was
> praying. (Mark 1:35)

In the Greek text, that final verb—"was praying"—is expressed in the imperfect tense, which denotes continued and/or repeated action. By using this verbal tense, Mark implies that Jesus spent a significant period of time occupied in that prayer. It began in the dark and ended after sunrise. That is to say, the Savior prayed through the transition from darkness to light.

We also know Jesus prayed through the transition from light to darkness—day to night. Mark writes of this phenomenon a bit later. The scene in question comes immediately after the multiplication of the loaves, an event that happened late in the day (Mark 6:35). Mark describes the apostles getting into their boat to sail away, while Jesus remains behind on the shore. He writes,

> And when he had sent them away, he departed to the mountain to pray. Now when evening came, the boat was in the middle of the sea; and he was alone on the land. (Mark 6:46–47)

In this text, the prayer of Jesus is said to begin in the light and continue into the darkness. It is not broken off until very late— "the fourth watch."[2] Thus, by way of sanctifying the structure of time, Jesus prays during the two daily transitions of light and darkness.

It is almost impossible to consider Jesus' preference for long nocturnal prayer without suspecting it was related to the vast expanse of the Palestinian sky at night. In that setting the Savior made his own the rapturous admiration of David, who, a thousand years before, prayed under that same spangled vault:

> Ki 'er'eh shaméka / ma'asé 'etsb'otéka / yaréha wekokabím 'ashér konántah—For I see Your heavens, / the work of Your fingers, / the moon and the stars, which You have appointed. (Psalm 8:3)

This "appointment" of the celestial bodies refers to the fourth day of Creation, on which "God made two great lights: the greater light to rule the day, and the lesser light to rule the night—and the stars" (Genesis 1:16). This nocturnal prayer of Jesus is set, then, not simply within the beauty of nature, but within the biblical narrative.

I do not mean by this simply the story told in Genesis, because the *original account* of Creation is much older than Genesis; it was already inscribed in the very stars, the structure of time and space. The "Book of Creation" is far more ancient than the book of Genesis. Genesis 1 simply tells *with* words what the Creation relates *without* words.

Creation itself speaks. Consequently, when Jesus prayed under the heavens, he not only *spoke* to God; he also *listened* because the moon and the stars—and also the sun—had a tale to tell:

> The heavens recount the glory of God,
> And the firmament declares the work of His hands.
> Day unto day tells the story,
> And night unto night reveals the knowledge.
>   (Psalm 19:1–2)

Indeed, the biblical author himself learned the story by doing what Jesus did—by listening closely to the subtle message of the stars:

> There is no speech or language
> where their voice is not heard.
> Their voice goes out into all the earth,
> and their words to the ends of the world. (Psalm 19:3–4)

Of all creatures on earth, only the human soul has the receptive capacity to attend to—to hear—the narrative declared in the heavens and—hearing it—to commune in prayer with the Creator revealed there. The Gospels testify that Jesus had frequent recourse to that communion, spending entire nights in such prayer: "He went out to the mountain to pray, and continued all night in prayer to God" (Luke 6:12).

We observed that the Evangelist Mark uses the imperfect tense (denoting continued/repeated action) to speak of Jesus' prayer. Night after night, Jesus went out under the stars to listen and to pray. Luke, going further, intensifies the same impression by recourse to an awkward periphrastic construction, difficult to render in comfortable English. Literally it reads, "He was remaining apart in the wilderness and praying" (Luke 5:16).

Inasmuch as we find Jesus praying this way from the very beginning of his public ministry, we are surely justified in thinking this form of prayer was already the habit of a lifetime. Indeed, we suspect it began in childhood; Jesus was able to read the heavens before he knew how to read the scrolls in the synagogue. We should think of the young Jesus standing under the stars, most of all, when we recall another line from Psalm 8: "Out of the mouths of babies and nursing infants / You have perfected praise."

THE TRANSFIGURATION

Four New Testament sources tell the story of Jesus transfigured on the mountain: the gospels of Matthew, Mark, and Luke, and the second epistle of Peter. In the following reflections we will concentrate on Luke and Peter, whose accounts of that singular event bring together themes pertinent to Jesus' self-understanding, especially the role of biblical prophecy.

There are several distinctive features about Luke's account of the Lord's Transfiguration. First is the time frame. Luke begins,

Now it came to pass, about eight days after these sayings, that
he took Peter, John, and James and went up on the mountain to
pray. (Luke 9:28)

Matthew (17:1) and Mark (9:2) both placed the Transfiguration
six days later, not eight. We should note that Luke does not say
"eight" either; he says *about* eight." Obviously, there is no historical contradiction between "six days" and "about eight days," but it
is worth remarking on Luke's change in the wording. Why did he
make this change?

It appears that the early Christians associated the event
of the Lord's Transfiguration with the Feast of Tabernacles
(*Sukkoth*), an association prompted by Peter's suggestion, "Let us
make three *tabernacles*." Indeed, the luminous cloud of which the
Gospels speak in the Transfiguration is to be associated with the
glorious cloud that filled the Tabernacle of the Lord's presence in
Numbers 9–10.

The association of the transfigured Lord with the Feast of
Tabernacles perhaps suggests why Luke changed the "six days" to
"about eight days." The Feast of Tabernacles does, in fact, last one
week and another day (Leviticus 23:34–36). Luke thus portrays
Jesus as *the* Tabernacle, the place where God and man meet.

A second distinctive feature of Luke's account is also found
in that same first verse of the story; namely, the detail that Jesus
"went up on the mountain *to pray*." Only Luke mentions the prayer
of Jesus in connection with the Transfiguration: "*As he prayed*, the
appearance of his face was altered."[3]

In other words, whereas Matthew and Mark portray the
Transfiguration as a religious experience of its three apostolic wit-
nesses—Peter, James, and John—Luke begins with *the experience of
Jesus* as he worshipped the Father on the mountain.

Third, only Luke among the Evangelists refers to Jesus speaking of his suffering and death within the Transfiguration account. Luke writes,

And behold, two men talked with him, who were Moses and Elijah, who appeared in glory and spoke of his *exodus* that he was going to fulfill (*pleroun*) at Jerusalem. (Luke 9:30–31)

Several features of this reference to the Passion are important to Luke's theological view of the Transfiguration:

First, Luke uses the technical theological expression *exodus* to speak of Jesus' coming death. In his choice of this special noun Luke conveys the soteriological significance of the Savior's death: It was an act of redemption from slavery. Jesus' sufferings and death delivered men from bondage. This is the meaning of the Greek word *exodus*.

Second, in his reference to Jesus' *exodus*, Luke explicitly places it "at Jerusalem." This, too, corresponds to a theme in Luke's gospel, where the Holy City is the culminating place of the narrative. Jerusalem is the city to which Jesus has steadfastly set his face to go.[4]

This motif was introduced early in Luke, when Anna the prophetess "spoke of him to all those who looked for redemption *in Jerusalem*" (Luke 2:38, emphasis added).

Third, by referring to the Savior's Passion within the Transfiguration story, Luke prepares for a later scene: the account of Jesus' agony. Only Luke will speak of that agony taking place—like the Transfiguration—on a mountain (Luke 22:39–41). As we shall consider when we come to the agony, both are scenes of prayer *on a mountain*, a motif strengthening the link between the Transfiguration and the Passion.

Fourth, in his picture of Moses and Elijah—the Law and the Prophets—discussing Jesus' *exodus* at Jerusalem, Luke touches a major theme of his theology—the fulfillment (*pleroun*) of Holy Scripture in Jesus' sufferings and death in Jerusalem.

In this respect, we will later consider the scene with the two disciples on the road to Emmaus, which will bring together the Passion and the fulfillment of Holy Scripture:

> Then he said to them, "O foolish ones, and slow of heart to believe in all that the prophets have spoken! Ought not the Christ to have suffered these things and to enter into his glory?" And beginning at Moses and all the Prophets, he expounded to them in all the Scriptures the things concerning himself. (Luke 24:25–27)

Here in the Transfiguration, then, Luke portrays Moses and Elijah talking with Jesus about the meaning of Holy Scripture. Jesus discusses with these major Old Testament characters his coming fulfillment of the Law and the Prophets, the very subject on which he will discourse to the two disciples on the road to Emmaus. These two disciples on the road to Emmaus symbolically correspond to Moses and Elijah here on the mountain.

Luke returns to this theme in the risen Jesus' final apparition in the upper room, where he affirms,

> These are the words which I spoke to you while I was still with you, that all things must be fulfilled [*plerothenai*] which were written in the Law of Moses and the Prophets and the Psalms concerning me. (Luke 24:44)

Luke's version of the Great Commission begins with this affirmation:

Thus *it is written*, and thus it was necessary for the Christ to suffer and to rise from the dead the third day, and that repentance and remission of sins should be preached in his name to all nations, beginning at Jerusalem. (24:46–47, emphasis added)

In the very context of the Great Commission, says Luke, "He opened their understanding, that they might comprehend the Scriptures" (24:45).

In Luke's account of the Transfiguration, then, the two representatives of the Law and the Prophets are described as discussing with Jesus his fulfillment of the Law and the Prophets. This scene on the mountain brings to perfection Jesus' early study of the Law and the Prophets in the synagogue at Nazareth.

JESUS AND PROPHECY

Jesus' Transfiguration, notably portrayed in the Synoptic Gospels, is also described in the second epistle of Peter. The latter tells the story with less detail but certainly with no less interest.

Peter begins,

Yes, I think it is right, as long as I am in this tent, to stir you up by reminding you, knowing that shortly I must put off my tent, just as our Lord Jesus Christ showed me. Moreover I will be careful to ensure that you always have a reminder of these things after my *exodus*. (1:13–15)

Peter's reference to his impending *exodus* indicates that this epistle was written sometime shortly before his martyrdom. The latter is traditionally dated during the persecution that followed Nero's fire at Rome in the summer of AD 64. After the blame for that fire was shifted onto the Christians of the city, the imperial police rounded up the Christians, along with their obvious leader, Peter, the chief of the apostles. He evidently wrote this letter while waiting to die.

Two words in this introduction seem especially pertinent to our theme.

First, Peter refers to his impending death as his *exodus*. This is the identical word Luke uses to speak of the conversation of Jesus with Moses and Elijah:

> And behold, two men talked with him, who were Moses and Elijah, who appeared in glory and spoke of his *exodus* which he was about to accomplish at Jerusalem. (Luke 9:30–31)

In the New Testament the word *exodus* refers to death in only two places—Luke and 2 Peter—both texts concerned with Jesus' Transfiguration.

Second, Peter speaks of his death in terms of putting off his "tent" or "tabernacle." Perhaps the associations attached to this metaphor provided the occasion for him to immediately speak of the Transfiguration; we recall from all three Synoptic Gospels that Peter had spoken enigmatically of "tents" on that occasion: "Let us make three *tents*: one for you, one for Moses, and one for Elijah."

In any case, the apostle immediately goes on to describe the event of the Transfiguration:

> For we did not follow cunningly devised fables when we made known to you the power and coming of our Lord Jesus Christ, but we were eyewitnesses of his majesty. For he received from God the Father honor and glory when such a voice came to him from the Excellent Glory: "This is My beloved Son, in whom I am well pleased." And we heard this voice, which came from heaven when we were with him on the holy mountain. (2 Peter 1:16–18)

There are several particulars to note about Peter's portrayal of the Transfiguration.

First, the lack of detail is clearly to be explained by the apostle's presumption that the event was already well-known to his readers. He was not obliged to elaborate on the details, beyond reminding his readers that he had been a witness to the event.

Second, his quality as a witness to the vision of glory and the Father's voice established Peter's authority to refute the "cunningly devised fables" that are the object of his concern throughout much of this epistle.[5]

Third, Jesus' Transfiguration confirmed the hopes of the ancient prophets, who desired to see what the apostles saw. Peter goes on to write,

> And so we have the prophetic word confirmed, which you do well to heed as a light that shines in a dark place, until the day dawns and the morning star rises in your hearts. (2 Peter 1:19)

The fulfillment of biblical prophecy in Christ is a personal preoccupation of the apostle Peter.[6]

Fourth, the "cunningly devised fables," concerning which Peter is so alarmed, have to do chiefly with the misinterpretation of biblical prophecy. Thus, in this context of the Transfiguration, he goes on to insist

> that no prophecy of Scripture is of any private interpretation, for prophecy never came by the will of man, but men spoke of God as they were moved by the Holy Spirit. (2 Peter 1:20–21)

That is to say, for Peter the Transfiguration was weighted with an exegetical significance, such as we have already seen in Luke's account of it; both versions of the story emphasize Jesus' fulfillment

of the Old Testament. The glory of the Transfiguration casts a con-
firming radiation on biblical prophecy. The true meaning of the
latter *comes to light* in the Transfiguration, where the apostles "have
the prophetic word confirmed."

All other interpretation of Holy Scripture, for Simon Peter,
consists in "cunningly devised fables." The glory of the transfigured Christ is the light of the Scriptures themselves, to which
Christians "do well to attend." This is their source of illumination
"until the day dawns and the morning star rises in your hearts."
The Bible's ultimate fulfillment comes in history's final revelation
of the transfigured Lord, "the bright morning star" (Revelation
22:16; cf. 2:28).

THE CHOICE OF THE TWELVE

The immediate social dimension of Jesus' prayer includes two subjects: first, Jesus and his disciples, and, second, the relationship of
his prayer to theirs. We take these in order.

First, Luke is the only New Testament writer who mentions
that Jesus—prior to choosing the twelve apostles from among his
disciples—spent the night in prayer:

> Now it came to pass in those days that he went out to the
> mountain to pray, and continued all night in prayer to God.
> And when it was day, he called his disciples to himself; and
> from them he chose twelve whom he also named apostles.
> (Luke 6:12–13)

Because it was a momentous task, the selection of these men
was made during Jesus' nightlong communion with his Father. As
he prayed during that night, did Jesus think carefully about each
of those particular men, mentioning them—one by one—to the

Father? The New Testament, by naming the apostles individually,[7] suggests that this was the case: anyway, it was in prayer that Jesus arrived at the choice of these men.

Indeed, in a later prayer to the Father, Jesus refers to that earlier night, during the course of which the apostolic selection was made:

> I have manifested Your name to the men whom You have given me out of the world. They were Yours; *You gave them to me.* (John 17:6, emphasis added)

The selection of these twelve inaugurated them to a special intimacy among the disciples. They were chosen to be—in a way unique to themselves—Jesus' friends:

> I have called you friends, for all things that I heard from my Father I have made known to you. You did not choose me, but I chose you. (John 15:15–16)

Jesus selected these men, first of all, to be *"with* him" (Mark 3:14). They were his *companions,* in the literal sense of sharing bread (*panis*) with him.

Perhaps this aspect of the apostolic selection is most pronounced in the gospel of John, where Jesus washes the feet of these friends and explains the significance of the act (John 13:1–17). Having chosen them within his prayer—his communion with the Father—he revealed the Father to these men, and he did this by being "with" them: "Have I been *with* you so long, and yet you have not known me, Philip? He who has seen me has seen the Father" (14:9, emphasis added).

Jesus' love for these men comes from God's love for him: "As the Father loved me, I also have loved you; abide in my love" (15:9).

Indeed, the Father loves them because they love Jesus: "the Father Himself loves you, because you have loved me" (16:27). Jesus' friendship with these men introduces them—in the measure that it can—to his personal intimacy with the Father.

Through his experience of prayer on the mountain during the night, Jesus' relationship to these men changed. He changed; they changed; everything between them changed. Jesus committed himself to these men, whom the Father gave him in prayer, and life began to move along a new path for all of them.

JESUS' PRAYER AND OURS

Second, Luke sets the giving of the Lord's Prayer in the context of Jesus' own prayer:

> Now it came to pass, as he was praying in a certain place—when he ceased—one of his disciples said to Him, "Lord, teach us to pray, as John also taught his disciples." So he said to them, "When you pray, say: 'Father, hallowed be Your name. Your kingdom come. Give us day by day our daily bread. And forgive us our sins, for we also forgive everyone who is indebted to us. And do not lead us into temptation.'" (Luke 11:1–4)

In this passage, Luke deliberately links the prayer of Christians to the prayer of Jesus; this formula of prayer is given at the request of a disciple who saw Jesus pray and wanted to know how to do it.

In Jewish liturgical worship, it was customary to address God as "Father." *Abinu, Malkinu*—"Our Father, our King"—has always been a standard praise formula in the synagogue. It is not surprising, therefore, that we find this form of address in the teaching of Jesus, even as we find it in his own prayer.[8]

In those instances in which Jesus addresses God as Father, however, the context and prayer convey an intimacy with God for which Judaism provides no real parallel. The term "Father" expresses the uniqueness of his relationship with God:

> I thank You, Father, Lord of heaven and earth, that You have hidden these things from the wise and prudent and revealed them to babies. Even so, Father, for so it seemed good in Your sight. All things have been delivered to me by my Father, and no one knows who the Son is except the Father, and who the Father is except the Son, and the one to whom the Son wills to reveal Him. (Luke 10:21–22)

And again,

> Father, I thank You that You have heard me. And I know that You always hear me, but because of the people who are standing by I said this, that they may believe that You sent me. (John 11:41–42)

And most of all,

> Father, I desire that they also whom You gave me may be with me where I am, that they may behold my glory which You have given me; for You loved me before the foundation of the world. (John 17:24)

Even as we reflect that such prayers point to the divinity of Christ and the Word's preexistence to created things, it is important to remember that it is a *human being* who speaks to God this way. This prayer springs from a human soul, takes shape in a human mind, and is expressed in human words. It is in a human consciousness that

God's Son is aware of "the glory which I had with You before the world was" (John 17:5).

When, in his sermons to the people, Jesus spoke of God as their Father, the ascription contained nothing to which his adversaries could object. No Pharisee would complain at being told, "Look at the birds of the air, for they neither sow nor reap nor gather into barns; yet your heavenly Father feeds them" (Matthew 6:26). Nor would the declaration, "Your heavenly Father knows that you need all these things" (6:32) give offense to the high priest. The Jewish leadership recognized these convictions as extensions of the teaching of the Torah and the Prophets.

It was quite another matter, however, to hear a Galilean carpenter say, "I am one who bears witness of myself, and the Father who sent me bears witness of me" (John 8:18). How could they endure to hear, "I do nothing of myself; but as my Father taught me, I speak these things"? (8:28). All along, these enemies had complained of what they saw as Jesus' casual attitude toward the law of the Sabbath, but this talk of God as *his* Father went much further:

> Therefore the Jews sought all the more to kill him, because
> he not only broke the Sabbath, but also said that God was his
> Father, making himself equal with God. (John 5:18)

The enemies of Jesus at least gave him the credit of meaning what he said. They admitted this much to Pilate:

> We have a Law, and according to the Law he ought to die, because
> he made himself the Son of God. (John 19:7)

When Jesus spoke of God as his "Father," it was the expression, not of an idea, but of an experienced relationship. In his communion with God—reflected particularly in prayer—he knew himself to be the Father's Son.

Consequently, it is important to consider these high assertions of Jesus as reflective of his experience in prayer. This interpersonal communion was the source of his assurance that "I and the Father are one" (John 10:30).

Thus, when Jesus spoke of God as "my Father," the expression was not a metaphorical reference; he was not saying, "God treats me like a father treats his son." "My Father" was not an external ascription that could be rephrased into some other intelligible form. The semantic force of "my Father," from the lips of Jesus, was unique, personal, and utterly literal. So used, "Father" was no figure of speech. The name "Father" expressed, rather, the unique and experienced relationship of Jesus to God. "*Abba*, Father" was the most perfect expression of Jesus' being. This man, Jesus of Nazareth, inwardly *knew* the Father—by being one with Him—in a way not otherwise available to human beings.

Indeed, no one could *know* Jesus as this Father knew him: "All things have been delivered to me by my Father, and no one knows the Son except the Father" (Matthew 11:27).

The astounding gift of Jesus to his disciples was the invitation to partake of his own intimacy with the Father. When he proclaimed, "Nor does anyone know the Father except the Son," he went on to add, "and the one to whom the Son chooses to reveal Him." This offer to share his relationship to the Father is the immediate context for Jesus' summons: "Come to me, all you who labor and are heavy laden, and I will give you rest" (Matthew 11:28).

Matthew's version of the Lord's Prayer conveys this relationship with the Father, the personal communion that Jesus shares with believers. The "our" of the "Our Father" forbids us to separate this prayer from Jesus' revelation of his Father to believers. This prayer cannot be abstracted from "the one to whom the Son chooses

to reveal Him." No one addresses God as *Abba* except by the power
and authority of that revelation by the Son. To be a "child of God"
means to partake—by divine grace and mercy—of Jesus' relationship to the Father. Thus, the "our" includes the believer's union with
Jesus in a common prayer to the Father. This was the summons
given at the final glorification of Jesus, when he spoke of "my Father
and your Father, my God and your God" (John 20:17).

8

JESUS AND THE WOMEN

FROM THE BEGINNING OF THESE REFLECTIONS, A MAJOR premise has been my persuasion that Jesus' maturing sense of mission and vocation was not something separable from the social tissue of his life—its organic particularity, the extended web of personal relationships by which he was bound to his countrymen and contemporaries and to their common history. Notwithstanding his partiality for solitary prayer, the Gospels do not portray Jesus as a hermit who made occasional visits into town. They picture him, on the contrary, as a prayerful man actively involved with real people and surrounded by friends and disciples.

Some of these specific and identified people were women.

For this reason, the title of the present reflection is chosen with particular attention to its definite article—*the* women. That is to say, our interest here is not in Jesus' relationship with women generally but with the particular women in whose company we find him—mother, friends, disciples, and beneficiaries of his mercy. These women appear to have been every bit as individual and unique as any of the apostles. The Good Shepherd called them *by name* (for example, Luke 10:41; John 20:16).

Summarizing the Christian female discipleship, Luke testifies that its company was not only numerous but also a source of concrete support in Jesus' ministry:

> He went through every city and village, preaching and bringing the glad tidings of the kingdom of God, and the Twelve with him, and certain women who had been healed of evil spirits and infirmities—Mary called Magdalene, out of whom had come seven demons, and Joanna the wife of Chuza, Herod's steward, and Susanna, and many others[1]—who provided for him from their resources. (Luke 8:1–3)

Luke's reference to the "seven demons" driven from Mary Magdalene (cf. Mark 16:9) prompts the suspicion that some of these women were the recipients of Jesus' healing and mercy. One thinks, for instance, of the "daughter of Abraham" whom Jesus healed in the synagogue, that lady "who had a spirit of infirmity eighteen years, and was bent over and could in no way straighten upright" (Luke 13:10–17). Then, there was another "daughter" who, until she touched the hem of his garment, had been hemorrhaging for twelve years (Luke 8:42–48). We recall, as well, the wife of Jairus, who watched Jesus raise her own daughter from the dead (Luke 8:49–56).

In addition to the Galilean women who traveled with him and the Twelve, we know of others associated with Jesus' ministry. They included the two sisters of Lazarus at Bethany—that family of which John observes, "Jesus loved Martha and her sister and Lazarus" (John 11:5).

Nor was his ministry limited to Jewish women. Both Mark (7:24–30) and Matthew (15:21–28) testify that he expelled a demon from the daughter of a Gentile woman, and John records a lengthy conversation with a woman of Samaria (John 4:6–26).

In some instances, the stories of these women, narrated in greater detail, call for a more detailed examination, which we will take up now.

A FUNERAL PROCESSION

Luke tells us that Jesus, arriving at the gate of a Galilean town called Nain, is accompanied not only by his regular disciples but also by a large crowd that follows him to the town. The village gateway is narrow, so these companions, endeavoring to enter, completely fill it (Luke 7:11–16).

Alas, the congestion at the gate is a disadvantage to a second group—also large—which is simultaneously trying to *leave* the town; this one is a funeral cortege, accompanying the body of a recently deceased young man. The two crowds encounter each other at the gate. One side, it would seem, must give way to the other . . . or is there a third option?

Actually, there is. Jesus walks up to the funeral procession and stops it:

> He went into a city called Nain; and many of his disciples went with him, and a large crowd. And when he came near the gate of the city, behold, a dead man was being carried out, the only son of his mother; and she was a widow. And a large crowd from the city was with her. When the Lord saw her, he had compassion on her and said to her, "Weep no more." Then he came and touched the open coffin, and the pallbearers stood still. And he said, "Young man, rise up, I tell you!" So he who was dead sat up and began to speak. And he presented him to his mother. (Luke 7:11–16)

Luke conveys the action of Jesus in this scene through five verbs: he *sees* the widow, he *feels* compassion for her, he *speaks*, he *touches* the bier, and he *presents* the risen son to his mother. Each of these is a human act, something done *in the flesh*.

First, Luke tells us, "the Lord *saw* her." The Gospels testify rather frequently that Jesus really did *see* people. Individual persons were not blurry and indistinct. He regarded them closely, attentive to their circumstances and needs. Thus, "Jesus *saw* Nathanael coming toward him" (John 1:47); he *saw* the paralytic lying at the pool of Bethesda (5:5–6); "he *saw* a man who was blind from birth" (9:1); he *saw* the sister's tears at the grave of Lazarus (11:33); and, as he hung on the cross, Jesus "*saw* his mother, and the disciple whom he loved standing by" (19:26).

This scene at Nain is one of three in which the Evangelist Luke speaks of Jesus *seeing* the special need and circumstances of individual women. The Nain story is profitably compared with the account of Jesus healing the crippled "daughter of Abraham" in the synagogue, where he first *sees* the woman in distress (Luke 13:12). Near the end of his ministry, Luke says, Jesus "looked up and saw the rich putting their gifts into the treasury, but he *saw* also a certain poor widow putting in two mites" (Luke 21:1–2; contrast Mark 12:42). Jesus' habit of personal observation and assessment—his imaginative perception of individual needs—is portrayed in the Gospels as the impetus of many blessings.

Second, says Luke, "He *had compassion* on her." The root of the action in this scene is Jesus' spontaneous gaze of sympathy. Not often does the New Testament identify Jesus' inner emotions, but this is one of the places.[2] Recognizing the dead man's mother as a widow with no other children—and, thus, no further means of support—Jesus seizes the hour.

Moreover, his compassion here is modified by a significant detail: the dead son is an *"only* child." In fact, this detail—only child—is a feature quite distinctive to Luke. The other gospels never use this expression to describe a beneficiary of Jesus' blessings. In Luke, however, this action at Nain is the first of three miracles

Jesus works for the benefit of parents of an "only child."[3] Luke also identifies the daughter of Jairus (Luke 8:42),[4] and the epileptic son (Luke 9:38)[5] as "only" children. This Lukan attention points to a particular social aspect of Jesus' compassion: his enhanced sympathy for parents who would lose an *only* child."

Third, Jesus *speaks*, first to the mother and then to her dead son. To each he speaks with authority: "Weep no more"[6] and "Young man, rise up, I tell you."

In all three gospel accounts of Jesus raising someone from the dead, he does so by speaking directly to the dead person. In addition to the present story, there are the instances of Jairus's daughter ("Darling, arise"—Mark 5:41) and Jesus' friend at Bethany ("Lazarus, come forth"—John 11:43).

In all three places, the voice of Christ is the instrument of resurrection:

> Amen, I say to you, the hour is coming, *and now is*, when the dead will hear the voice of the Son of God; and those who hear will live. (John 5:25)

Fourth, Jesus "came and *touched* the open coffin," at which point "the pallbearers stood still." Here we have more than a traffic jam at a village gateway; this funeral march, this procession to the cemetery, goes no further. It is *over*. The funeral is called off.

Luke takes special care here to portray the living Jesus as triumphant over death. Hence, it is significant that he refers to Jesus in this story as *the Lord*: "When *the Lord* saw her." Now, this term "Lord"—*ho Kyrios*—is the title by which the early Christians normally designated the risen Messiah, victorious over death and the grave:

> Therefore let all the house of Israel know assuredly that God has made this Jesus, whom you crucified, both Lord and Christ. (Acts 2:36)[7]

Although the Bethlehem angels had called Jesus "the *Lord* Messiah" (Luke 2:11), the scene at Nain is the first time Luke uses his narrator's voice to refer to Jesus by this important title. From this point on, Luke will frequently speak of Jesus as "the *Lord*."[8] That is to say, the victory over death at Nain is a turning point in the Lukan narrative; from here on in Luke's account, Jesus is *Lord*.

Fifth, referring to the dead son, Luke says that Jesus "presented him to his mother." This clause, which repeats word-for-word the Greek text of 1 Kings 17:23, puts the reader in mind of the prophet Elijah, who raised the "only son" of the widow of Zarephath (cf. Luke 4:25). Evidently the witnesses of this miracle also thought of that earlier story about a prophet because they exclaimed, "A great *prophet* has risen among us."

This story of the widow's son, found only in Luke, serves the overall integrity and message of his gospel. By inserting it into the narrative sequence he inherited from Mark, Luke prepares the reader for the inquiry Jesus will soon receive from John the Baptist: "Are You the Coming One, or do we look for another?" (Luke 7:20). Jesus' response to John's query will include the detail, "dead people are raised" (7:22). Luke's insertion of the event at Nain serves to justify the response that Jesus sends back to John.

JACOB'S WELL

Only John tells us what Jesus did at the Samaritan well:

> So he came to a city of Samaria, which is called Sychar, near the plot of ground that Jacob gave to his son Joseph. Now Jacob's well was there. Jesus therefore, being wearied from his journey, sat thus by the well. It was about the sixth hour. A woman of Samaria came to draw water. Jesus said to her, "Give me a drink." For his disciples had gone away into the city to buy food. (John 4:5–8)

The woman is surprised at the request—or at least pretends to be—for two reasons: First, the culture of the day discouraged a man from addressing an unknown woman. Second, Jews generally avoided dealings with Samaritans. Both objections are conveyed in her answer: "How is it that *you*, being a *Jew*, ask a drink from *me*, a *Samaritan woman?*" (John 4:9, emphasis added).

Thus begins a lengthy dialogue, in which Jesus offers to give this woman "living water," a theological metaphor she is unable to grasp (John 4:1–15). Then, by way of being practical and getting down to business, he tells her, "Go, call your husband, and come here" (4:16). Jesus knows, of course, that she has no husband, a fact she readily admits. And here Jesus comes to the nub of the woman's moral state:

> You have well said, "I have no husband," for you have had five
> husbands, and the one whom you now have is not your husband;
> in that you spoke truly. (John 4:17–18)

Now the discussion turns very practical, indeed!

When Jesus requested that the woman bring her husband, he was quite aware of her dubious marital situation. His request to the woman was an example of rhetorical pretense.

Indeed, this "request" was of a piece with Jesus' occasional recourse to the rhetorical device known as *erotema*, something said—or more often asked—for the hidden purpose of soliciting reflection and/or taking a conversation in a particular direction. As we shall see later, this device was especially adept for springing a surprise.[9]

Put on the spot this way, our Samaritan lady decides to pose another theological question, this one less . . . well, personal:

> Sir, I perceive that you are a prophet. Our fathers worshiped on
> this mountain, and you say that in Jerusalem is the place where
> one ought to worship. (John 4:19–20)

There ensues a further conversation on the point of proper worship, and then, in reply to the woman's comment about the Messiah, Jesus tells her, "I who speak to you am he" (John 4:21–26).

The discussion comes abruptly to an end when the apostles arrive, and the Samaritan woman hurries off to tell her fellow citizens about the stranger she encountered at the well: "Come, see a man who told me all things that I ever did. Could this be the Messiah?" (4:29). When she introduces them to Jesus, they reach some conclusions of their own:

> Now we believe, not because of what you said, for we ourselves have heard, and we know that this is indeed the Savior of the world. (John 4:42)

John's story of the Samaritan woman—a story he surely knew from the lady's own account—portrays a growth in her faith. As the narrative progresses, we observe a development in her understanding of Jesus, a development indicated in the various ways she addresses him. When she first meets Jesus, he is called simply "a Jew" (John 4:9).

This is important to the story as a whole because Jesus himself will presently declare, "Salvation is of the Jews" (4:22). On this woman's lips, nonetheless, the designation "Jew" indicates two things: First, it says that she assesses Jesus only within a certain class of people. He is not yet a distinguishable person. And second, the word *Jew* indicates the woman's sense of separation from Jesus, because "Jews have no dealings with Samaritans."

Next, she addresses Jesus as "Sir" (John 4:11; presumably the Aramaic *Mar*). The woman is making a significant step here in terms of personal respect. It indicates a change of attitude of her part. Then, within four verses "Sir" becomes "prophet" (4:19), when Jesus directs the woman's attention to her own moral failings. The conversation next takes a new bound forward when Jesus identifies himself as the Messiah. Finally, when the other Samaritans meet him, he is called "the Savior of the world." This is a considerable doctrinal development within a single story!

The woman from Samaria has now come a long way. Starting out that day, hardly suspecting what lay ahead, she laboriously carried her sins to the well, where she met a Jew, who asked her for a drink of water. The Jew presently became a "Sir," and then a "prophet" who reminded her that she was a sinner. No matter, though, for he did not press the point. He was, after all, the Messiah. And because this Messiah was likewise the Savior of the world, he knew exactly what to do with her sins.

A GENTILE

One of the most striking—and challenging—encounters in Jesus' life was his meeting with a Gentile woman north of Galilee. Matthew describes her approach:

> Then Jesus went out from there and departed to the region of Tyre and Sidon. And behold, a woman of Canaan came from that region and cried out to him, saying, "Have mercy on me, O Lord, Son of David! My daughter is severely demon-possessed." (Matthew 15:21–22)

So many gospel stories start this way: a person comes to Jesus—a blind man, say, or a leper, or a centurion concerned about his son—and this person is invariably helped, most often without delay. Consequently, the reader expects Jesus simply to tell this woman, "Why, certainly, go your way, your daughter is healed."

Instead, Matthew informs us, "But he answered her not a word."

Oof, this is tough! The woman persists in her request, however, to the distress of the disciples, who "came and urged him, saying,

'Send her away, for she cries out after us'" (Matthew 15:23).[10] And, as though the woman were not sufficiently discouraged, Jesus says to her, "I was not sent except to the lost sheep of the house of Israel" (Matthew 15:24). At this point, we Gentile readers can hardly believe our ears!

This woman, however, just will not give up: "'Then she came and prostrated before him, saying, 'Lord, help me!'" (Matthew 15:25). The scene is becoming embarrassing. Can things get worse?

Yes, they can—and do: "But he answered and said, 'It is not good to take the children's bread and throw it to the puppies.'" Oh, my! Is Jesus calling this Gentile a dog? No wonder the gospel of Luke does not relate this story!

Then, all of a sudden, the story changes, and it is the woman who changes it. Like Jesus' mother at Cana, she gets pushy with the Savior: "Yes, Lord," she responds, "yet even the puppies eat the crumbs which fall from their masters' table."

In the end, of course, "her daughter was healed from that very hour" (Matthew 15:28), but the reader may be left with the feeling that the whole transaction was excessively painful and that Jesus, at least for a while, was acting terribly out of character. What should be said about this?

Not for a moment do I believe Jesus was insulting this woman. Once again, I take his silence and then his reference to puppies as a rhetorical pretense, very much like his request that the Samaritan woman should summon her husband.

What was Jesus' purpose here? In Matthew's gospel he clearly intended to try this woman's faith. Indeed, it is her faith that he recommends: "Ma'am, great *is* your *faith*! Let it be to you as you desire" (Matthew 15:28, emphasis added). A friend of mine once compared this lady's faith to that of Abraham, as he "haggled a price" with God over the fate of Sodom.

That is to say, rhetorical considerations provide the key to the conversation between Jesus and this Gentile woman. Perhaps this point is more clearly expressed in Mark's version of the story, where she is known as "a Greek, a Syro-Phoenician by birth" (Mark 7:26).

In Mark's account, the woman is praised not for her faith but for her "word"—her manner of expression: *dia touton ton logon*. Jesus admits that this woman has bested him in the conversation! He tells her, in effect, "Ma'am, you certainly have a way with words." Jesus recognizes the good logic and superior style in which the woman humbly asserts, "Even the puppies under the table eat from the children's crumbs." The lady is not only persistent; she is also eloquent. And Jesus is . . . well, impressed!

A DESPERATE CASE

As the Savior begins to walk toward the home of Jairus—where he will raise that man's daughter from the dead—a large crowd of followers is pressing around him. Hiding within this crowd is a woman who, strictly speaking, is not supposed to be there, mixing indiscriminately with other people. She is ritually unclean.

Twelve years earlier, this woman began to have her period, something that she had taken as normal since about the age of twelve. She did not worry about this; it was a scheduled inconvenience, as it were, a nuisance at best, something women had experienced ever since the day Eve took that first bite of the forbidden fruit. She was confident, however, that the bleeding would be over in a few days.

Meanwhile, this lady recognized a social fact: she was ritually impure, according to the Mosaic Law. And as ritually impure, she suffered a measure of monthly ostracism: For instance, she did not eat at the common table with her family during this time. She was forbidden, moreover, to prepare the family's meals. She slept alone and was prohibited from touching her husband and children for a few days. The details were all worked out in the Torah. It would be over soon; the proper sacrifice would be offered, and she could return to her normal life and routine.

Much to her chagrin, the bleeding did not stop. It continued for a whole month, and then a second month, and then a third. At some point she consulted physicians about the problem, but to no avail. Indeed, according to the gospel of Mark, her consultation with the doctors actually made things worse—a detail curiously omitted by "the beloved physician," the Evangelist Luke!

By the end of the year, the lady was in terrible shape. She suffered from severe anemia from the loss of blood and iron. Her nerves were on edge. She had not touched another human being in twelve months. Instead of enduring ostracism for a few days, she started to suffer the emotional ravages of total isolation.

Her responses grew erratic and strange, as depression became chronic. By the end of a year, the woman's self-image and sense of personal dignity were severely impaired. But a second year followed, and this one much worse.

Let us not regard this woman as a fictional character in one of Jesus' parables. She is a real person, whose very soul and body are being destroyed by a condition over which she has no control. By the time we find her in the gospel story,[11] this lady has suffered the trauma and devastation of her condition for twelve whole years. Meanwhile, her children have grown up, and now she has grandchildren, whom she is forbidden to touch. Life is passing her by, and her sole hope is that it will pass by quickly.

She is bent and beaten. Those who knew her could say, "Who has believed our report? There is no beauty in her. She is despised and rejected of men, a woman of sorrows and acquainted with grief. We turned our faces, as it were, away from her. She is smitten by God and afflicted."

Like Job, she longs to die—anything to escape the fate in which her hopeless existence is reduced to the confines of a coffin: sick beyond measure, emotionally isolated, physically weak, unable to think clearly, totally listless in mind and body, and deprived of elementary hope—a skeleton of herself.

Nonetheless, the lady has, of late, heard a rumor about the wonder-worker, Jesus of Nazareth. There is word on the street that healings have been conveyed by the mere touch of his clothing (Matthew 14:36).

Clinging desperately to this final chance of deliverance, she resolves even to violate the Law by hiding herself in a crowd. Unnoticed, she inches forward to the point where her extended finger, reaching through the closely packed mass of other bodies, can barely touch the hem of Jesus' garment. "And immediately," says Luke, "her flow of blood stopped" (8:44). She feels the sudden surge of health rushing into her wasted frame. The trauma of twelve years is over!

Yes, it is over, but something new is just about to begin. This lady is not the only one who *feels* something when Jesus' garment is touched. Jesus, also, perceives that power—*dynamis*—has gone out from him, and he is unwilling to let the matter lie. Turning about, he declares, "*Somebody* touched me, for I perceived power going out from me."

Indeed, *somebody*. For twelve years this woman has thought of herself as a nobody, but to Jesus she is somebody. He will not permit her to be concealed, lost, and absorbed in a crowd. She has an identity. She is *somebody*! Now healed in body by the physical act of touching, she must begin the healing of her spirit by being spoken to and reassured.

So, he who calls each of his sheep by name requires the lady to come forward and be *identified*. Now, says Luke,

when the woman saw that she was not hidden, she came trembling; and falling down before him, she declared to him in the presence of all the people the reason she had touched him and how she was healed immediately. (Luke 8:47)

Jesus then declares the word of personal reassurance, which begins the healing of her soul: "Daughter, your faith has saved you. Go in peace."

It is legitimate to wonder what the lady thought of this reference to her faith. She probably felt she had no faith at all. In her case, faith had disguised itself as desperation. Yet, weak as it was— no larger than a mustard seed—this faith had filled the finger she placed on the fringe of Jesus' robe. It had been sufficient; the mountain was moved and thrown into the sea.

TWO SCENES IN BETHANY

Although Jesus sometimes spoke reproachfully to his disciples (cf. Mark 8:17–21, 33), he was reluctant, it seems, to let anyone else do so. Thus, we find him, on occasion, defending these disciples against their critics and enemies (Luke 5:33–35; 6:1–5). The most notable instance, surely, involved Jesus' concern for their safety at the moment of his arrest: "If you seek me, let these go their way" (John 18:8).

Jesus' instinct to protect his loved ones extended in a special way to the women. In the Gospels we find not a single example of someone criticizing a woman in Jesus' presence and getting away with it.

The Gospels are emphatic on this point. For instance, on the occasion when he restored a crippled woman in the synagogue, Jesus became incensed and shouted "Hypocrite!" to the synagogue leader who embarrassed the woman and blamed *her* for being healed on the Sabbath (Luke 13:10–16).

Likewise, Jesus was quick to defend a sinful woman against the self-righteous sneers of a Pharisee named Simon (Luke 7:36–50).

Most memorable, perhaps, was the occasion when he put to shame the accusers of an adulteress (John 8:2–11).

We know of two instances when Jesus came to the defense of Mary of Bethany, one of those three siblings of whom we are told, "Now Jesus loved Martha and her sister and Lazarus" (John 11:5).

The first of these stories—recorded by Luke (10:38–42)—describes the time when Jesus came to "a certain village, and a certain woman named Martha welcomed him into her house." This last detail is important: Jesus came to *Martha's* house. Martha was in charge, and, to make Jesus feel welcome, she went to great pains, "distracted by all the preparations that had to be made" (Luke 10:40).

As the day wore on, and the finishing times for the various dishes started to converge—the salad to be mixed, the roasted corn to be stirred, the fish to be cut, the cups to be filled, the table to be set, and the bread to come out of the oven—Martha's dedicated industry began to assume a note of impatience. One of the reasons she was so busy—or at least according to Martha—was that this younger sister of hers was not helping with the chores: "Mary, seated at the feet of Jesus, was listening[12] to his word."

When Martha felt she could endure it no more, she mentioned this concern to their guest: "Lord, do you not care that my sister has left me to serve alone? Tell her, then, to give me a hand." That is to say, Martha accused her sister of wasting time when there was work to be done. It must have seemed to her a perfectly reasonable concern, and Jesus, she was confident, would certainly agree.

To her consternation, however, his response not only defended Martha's sister but went on to assert the *superiority* of Mary's peaceful occupation:

Martha, Martha, you are worried and troubled about many things. But only one thing is necessary. Mary has chosen the better[13] portion, which will not be taken away from her. (Luke 10:41–42)

In order to understand how Mary's occupation represented the "better portion," it is useful to consider her activity—sitting and listening to Jesus' word—within the context of Luke's larger story. For starts, this description supports a comparison of Mary of Bethany with Jesus' own mother, who "kept all these things and pondered them in her heart" (Luke 2:19, 51).

Both Jesus' mother and Mary of Bethany are portrayed as true contemplatives, who embody the model described in the parable of the sower. In Luke's version of that parable, the seeds "that fell on the good ground are those who, having heard the word with a noble and good [agathe] heart, keep it and bear fruit with patience" (Luke 8:15). For Luke, that is to say, true contemplation involves the hearing of God's word in purity of heart. For Luke, both Jesus' mother and Mary of Bethany are portrayed as occupied with the "one thing necessary."

Jesus' second defense of Mary of Bethany is narrated by John (12:1–8). It was she, John tells us, who, just six days before the Passover, "took a pound of very costly oil of spikenard, anointed the feet of Jesus, and wiped his feet with her hair."

Whereas in the former story, Mary was reprimanded for wasting time, in the present instance she is accused of wasting money. Her critic now is none other than Judas Iscariot, that famous apostolic bookkeeper and efficiency expert, a man who knew a thing or two about finances: "Why was this fragrant oil not sold for three hundred silver pieces and given to the poor?"

John, the narrator, aware that Judas is about to sell Jesus out for a fraction of that amount, lets his readers in on a dirty little secret: Judas, he explains, "said this, not that he cared for the poor, but because he was a thief, and had the money box; and he used to take what was put in it."

The reader is struck by Jesus' restraint in this story. He says very little here to Judas Iscariot, even though he knew "it was he who would betray Him, being one of the twelve" (John 6:71). Jesus does, however, defend Mary of Bethany by placing her action in the context of the murder to which Judas's betrayal will lead: "Let her be, that she may preserve it for the day of my burial."

Whereas the first story contrasts Mary's "better portion" with the good activities of her sister, this second story opposes her loving generosity with the evil being plotted by Judas.

AN *OFFICIAL* LINK

Alone among the four Evangelists, Luke tells the story of Jesus' judicial appearance before Herod Antipas on the day of the Crucifixion (23:6–12).

This is the same Herod whom Luke mentions closer to the beginning of his gospel, at the inauguration of the ministry of John the Baptist (3:1). Thus, in Luke's literary construction, these two references to Herod Antipas serve to frame Jesus' public ministry, which, as that Evangelist was careful to note, extended to

all the time that the Lord Jesus went in and out among us, beginning from the baptism of John to that day when he was taken up from us. (Acts 1:21–22)

Luke also tells how the animosity of Herod Antipas toward Jesus (cf. Luke 13:31) was later directed against Jesus' disciples (cf. Acts 12:1, 11). Indeed, Luke regarded the collusion of Antipas and Pontius Pilate, which was sealed at Jesus' trial (Luke 23:12), as the fulfillment of David's prophecy (Psalm 2:1–2) of the gathering of the world's leaders "against the Lord and against His Christ" (Acts 4:25–27).

It is significant that Luke, when he tells us of Jesus' appearance before Antipas on Good Friday, does more than state the bare event. He goes into some detail about how

> Herod, with his men of war, treated him with contempt and
> mocked him, arrayed him in a gorgeous robe, and sent him back
> to Pilate. (Luke 23:11)

This description implies that Luke had access to an eyewitness account of the event, an event at which, as far as we know, no Christian disciple was present. The historian rightly inquires how Luke knew all this.

Moreover, in addition to these external items of the narrative, Luke even addresses the motive and internal dispositions of Antipas, saying that

> he was exceedingly glad; for he had desired for a long time to see
> him, because he had heard many things about him, and he hoped
> to see some miracle done by him. (23:8)

Once again the historian properly wonders how Luke was privy to these sentiments. What was his source for this material, a source apparently not available to the other Evangelists?

Luke himself provides a hint toward answering this historical question when he mentions a certain Chuza, described as a "steward" of Herod Antipas. The underlying Greek noun here is *epitropos*, the same word that refers to the vineyard foreman in Matthew 20:8, but in the Lukan context it more likely points to a high political office, such as a chief of staff.

It does not tax belief to imagine that such a person would be present at Jesus' arraignment before Herod Antipas. Indeed, this would be exactly the sort of person we would expect to be present on that occasion, when Herod was in Jerusalem to observe the Passover. Furthermore, Chuza is also the sort of person we would expect to be familiar with Herod's own thoughts, sentiments, and motives with respect to Jesus.

And how did Chuza's information come to Luke? Most certainly through Chuza's wife, Joanna, whom Luke includes among the Galilean women who traveled with Jesus and the apostles, providing for him "from their substance" (Luke 8:3). Joanna, whom Luke is the only Evangelist to mention by name, was surely his special channel of information that only he, among the Evangelists, seems to have had. Married to a well-placed political figure in the Galilean court, Joanna was apparently a lady of some means, who used her resources to provide for the traveling ministry of Jesus and the apostles. Acting in this capacity, she must have been very well-known among the earliest Christians. Only Luke, however, speaks of her by name, a fact that seems to indicate that he had interviewed her in the composition of his gospel.

We can guess that Joanna's adherence to Jesus was not without its difficulties for her domestic life. Here she was, the wife of a high political official, providing support for someone who would die as a political criminal.

Her loyalty was supremely rewarded, however, because the risen Lord saw fit to number Joanna among the holy myrrh-bearers, those surprised women who "came to the tomb bringing the spices which they had prepared," found the stone rolled away from the tomb, then prostrated before the two herald angels of the Pascha, and subsequently "told these things to the apostles" (Luke 24:1, 5–7, 10). One suspects that Joanna also had a thing or two to tell her husband, Chuza, later that day. In her adherence to Jesus, she had put all her eggs in one basket; it turned out to be the Easter basket.

9

THE GROWING CRISIS

AS WE HAVE REFLECTED BEFORE, JESUS' PUBLIC MINISTRY did not last long, not much over two years. It is neither easy to say when animosity toward him began to rise, nor to gauge accurately the course of its growth, but Mark's account suggests it happened early.

In this account, Jesus' ministry has barely begun when Mark writes of five situations of conflict with critics: (1) the healing of the paralytic in 2:1–12;[1] (2) Jesus' eating with sinners in 2:13–17; (3) a question about fasting in 2:18–22; (4) the Sabbath observance in 2:23–28; and (5) the healing of a man's crippled hand in 3:1–5.

Promptly after this fifth incident, Mark tells us, "the Pharisees went out and immediately plotted with the Herodians against Him, how they might destroy Him" (Mark 3:6). Thus, in Mark's gospel the entire ministry of Jesus is conducted under the cloud of a death warrant.

The indictments against Jesus were multiple: First, not only did he take a fairly flexible approach to the Sabbath rest,[2] but he even claimed to be "Lord of the Sabbath."[3] Second, Jesus asserted authority, on at least two occasions, to forgive sins.[4] Third, Jesus imposed his will on the customary procedures in the temple.[5]

Fourth, "he taught them as one having authority, and not as the scribes" (Matthew 7:29). Fifth, and most significant, "he not only broke the Sabbath, but also said that God was his Father, making himself equal with God" (John 5:18).

A true crisis in Jesus' work seems to have developed near the beginning of its second year. It was at the halfway point in his ministry—its second Passover (John 6:4), one year before his execution—that "many of his disciples backed off and walked with him no more" (6:66). Also, it was at that time, John tells us, that Jesus foresaw which of the disciples would be his betrayer (6:70–71).

It is reasonable to date, at this period, the first two of Jesus' predictions of those things that would, in the end, befall him in Jerusalem. It was then that Jesus "began" to talk about the terrible things that would befall him (Mark 8:31; 9:30–31).

Later that year, when Jesus visited the Holy City during other feast days—Sukkoth in September (John 7:2–11) and Hanukkah in December (10:22)—everyone recognized his life was in danger (7:1; 10:31).

In the spring of the following year, consequently, when Jesus announced his intention to return to Judea once again, those who accompanied him were understandably dismayed. Two gospels record the reaction.

John:

Then after this he said to the disciples, "Let us go to Judea again." The disciples said to him, "Rabbi, the Jews lately sought to stone you, and are you going there again?" (John 11:7–8)

Mark:

Now they were on the road, going up to Jerusalem, and Jesus was going before them; and they were amazed. And as they followed, they were afraid. Then he took the twelve aside again and began to tell them the things that would happen to him: "Behold, we are going up to Jerusalem, and the Son of Man will be betrayed to the chief priests and to the scribes; and they will condemn him to death and deliver him to the Gentiles; and they will mock him, and scourge him, and spit on him, and kill him." (Mark 10:32–34)

The immediate purpose of Jesus' return south was to raise up his friend Lazarus, who had just died (John 11:11–15). The apostle Thomas (whom we will consider later and at greater length) sensed the impending tragedy: "Let us also go, that we may die with him" (11:16).

After the raising of Lazarus, Jesus' enemies went berserk:

Then the chief priests and the Pharisees gathered a council and said, "What shall we do? For this Man works many signs. If we let him alone like this, everyone will believe in him, and the Romans will come and take away both our place and nation." And one of them, Caiaphas, being high priest that year, said to them, "You know nothing at all, nor do you consider that it is expedient that one man should die for the people, and not that the whole nation should perish." Then, from that day on, they plotted to put him to death. (John 11:47–50, 53)

Jesus' enemies so thoroughly "lost it" at this time that they "plotted to put Lazarus to death also" (John 12:10). With such homicidal craziness abounding in Jerusalem, Jesus determined to stay away until the week before Passover. He lodged with friends in the suburbs (John 11:54–57).

When he finally did enter Jerusalem, Jesus was careful to do so in the safety of numbers. His entrance, which took on the character of a triumphant march, was virtually a challenge.[6]

Open conflicts with enemies continued to preoccupy Jesus through the first half of the ensuing week, apparently in the temple vicinity. Arrest in the temple would be difficult because of the large crowds, swollen by the thousands of pilgrims who had come to the city for Passover.

According to Mark's description of these days, Jesus argued with various enemies who sought to trap him into some punishable offense: (1) "the chief priests, the scribes, and the elders," who questioned his authority to reform the temple proceedings (Mark 11:27–33); (2) "the Pharisees and the Herodians," who tested him with respect to paying Roman taxes (12:13–17); (3) "Sadducees, who say there is no resurrection" (12:18–27); (4) "one of the scribes" with a question about the greatest commandment in the Torah (12:28–34); and (5) with his enemies generally, a question about a Davidic reference to the Messiah (12:35–37). These five conflict stories during Jesus' final week correspond to Mark's list of the five other conflicts at the beginning of the Savior's ministry (Mark 2:1–3:5).

Thus, those several days before Passover, which Mark chronicles with remarkable precision,[7] were spent in the company of large crowds, a circumstance that made Jesus' arrest difficult (Mark 12:12; Luke 22:2). Hired spies were everywhere (Luke 20:20), and Jesus was cautious:

> And in the daytime he was teaching in the temple, but at night he went out and stayed on the mountain called Olivet. Then early in the morning all the people came to him in the temple to hear him. (Luke 21:37–38; cf. Mark 11:11)

Jesus' enemies' best chance to seize him was to bribe one of his intimates into a betrayal. This task proved to be very easy. They were approached on Wednesday of that week by a volunteer, who inquired, "What are you willing to give me if I deliver him to you?" They fixed on a sum—thirty pieces of silver, the price of a slave (Exodus 21:32)—and the betrayer "sought opportunity to betray him" (Matthew 26:14–16). That opportunity would come during the next night—Thursday.

Prior to examining the betrayal by Judas, however, let us back up a bit and reflect on a few earlier episodes in this mounting crisis.

THE PARALYTIC WITH THE RESOURCEFUL FRIENDS

In all three Synoptic Gospels, the healing of the paralytic[8] is promptly followed by the calling of the tax collector and Jesus' meal with sinners.[9] Since these stories all deal with the same theme—Jesus' relationship to sin and sinners—it is likely that their sequence reflects an early catechetical pattern, perhaps even a chronological memory.

In Mark's gospel, the incident of the paralytic is also the earliest example of Jesus' conflict with enemies. Mark's version of the story is arguably the most colorful:

> And again [Jesus] entered Capernaum after some days, and it was heard that he was in the house. Immediately many gathered together, so that there was no longer room to receive them, not even near the door. And he preached the word to them. Then they came to him, bringing a paralytic who was carried by four men. And when they could not come near him because of the crowd, they uncovered the roof where he was. So when they had broken through, they let down the pallet on which the paralytic was lying. (Mark 2:1–4)

At this point in the story, Mark turns the reader's attention away from this unusual sight and directs it to Jesus. If the dangling descent of the paralytic was dramatic, no less so was the voice of the

Savior, reacting to the sight. Carefully looking at the situation, Jesus was able to discern three things:

First, observing the men lowering the paralytic, "Jesus *saw their faith.*" He looked past the act to the motive. Here we detect one of Jesus' truly unique traits, the spiritual ability to discern faith, or unbelief, in the hearts of those he met. This event is Mark's first example of it.

Second, Jesus was able to discern the spiritual state of the paralytic himself: "He said to the paralytic, 'Son, your sins are forgiven you.'" Whereas he sees faith in the paralytic's supporters, he sees sin in the paralytic.

It is worth remarking that, although there are no references to personal sins in the gospel stories about Jesus cleansing lepers or restoring sight to the blind or curing other sorts of ailments, he mentions sin in the present instance and in one other case of a paralytic (John 5:1–15).

Is there perhaps some aspect of paralysis itself that serves as an allegory of sin, something about the affliction that narrates the properties of sin? Perhaps so. The reader's curiosity is aroused, anyway. Although Jesus denied that the blind man had sinned (John 9:3), he intimates the presence of sin in two paralytics.

What *is* clear is the way those in attendance reacted to Jesus' assertion of authority to forgive sins:

And some of the scribes were sitting there and reasoning in their hearts, "Why does this man speak blasphemies like this? Who can forgive sins but God alone?" (Mark 2:6–7)

Third, Jesus could read their hostile thoughts:

But immediately, when Jesus perceived in his spirit that they reasoned thus within themselves, he said to them, "Why do you reason about these things in your hearts?" (Mark 2:8)

In short, Mark lists three things—secret things—that Jesus discerns in this scene: the faith of the friends, the sins of the paralytic, the thoughts of his critics.

Then Jesus, in order to demonstrate his authority to forgive sins, commands the paralytic, "I say to you, arise, take up your bed, and go to your house." At this point, the man, now healed of his paralysis, climbs off the pallet, detaches it from the cords by which it is hung, rolls it up, takes it up, and carries it home (Mark 2:5–12).

It is noteworthy that the first objection to Jesus' ministry was directed not to his alleged violation of the Sabbath but to his affirmation of personal authority to do what only God can do: forgive sins. This offense his enemies call "blasphemy," the very charge they will bring against him at his trial before the Sanhedrin (Mark 14:62). The story of the paralytic, therefore, is an early introduction of Jesus' trial. In this respect, the rest of Mark's gospel can be read as a transcript, as it were, of that trial.

By the end of this initial group of five controversies, the enemies of Jesus will already have decided to seek the death penalty: "Then the Pharisees went out and immediately plotted with the Herodians against Him, *how they might destroy Him* [*pos avton apolesosin*]" (Mark 3:6). The Greek expression here is identical to that used later to speak of the resolve of Jesus' enemies, just days before his execution. Right after his purging of the temple, Mark tells us, "the scribes and chief priests heard it and sought *how they might destroy Him* [*pos avton apolesosin*]" (Mark 11:18). This verbal correspondence corroborates the impression that Mark's entire gospel is a sort of extended account of the Passion.

SON AND HEIR

The parable of the vine growers—listed prominently in Jesus' teaching during the last week of his earthly life—provides a sharp, defining outline of how he came to understand not only his ministry to his contemporaries but also his larger significance in the history of Israel. It illustrates how Jesus thought about his mission and destiny. No other of his parables, I believe, contains such an obviously "autobiographical" perspective.

This parable of the vine growers, in which the sending of God's Son is presented as the defining moment of history, may be regarded as an extension of what Jesus said when he first preached on Isaiah in the synagogue at Nazareth: "Today this Scripture is fulfilled in your hearing" (Luke 4:21). In the story of the vinegrowers, we see the clearest evidence that Jesus addressed, in his own heart, the large dimensions of his destiny.

The three forms of the vine growers' parable[10] differ slightly in details, but the overall structure of the story is identical in each of them. We will stick to that structure, even as we look at details in all three versions.

First, God created Israel and put certain people in charge:

> There was a certain landowner who planted a vineyard and set a hedge around it, dug a winepress in it and built a tower. And he leased it to vinedressers and went into a far country. (Mathew 21:33)

When Jesus addressed this parable to the men who plotted to kill him (Matthew 21:45–46), those Jewish scholars of the Law and the Prophets could hardly fail to recognize, in these initial details, the story's resemblance to a lyrical poem of the prophet Isaiah eight centuries before. Perhaps some of them knew Isaiah's poem by heart. It begins, in lines of incomparable beauty,

> A song of my beloved regarding his vineyard—
> *'ashírah n'a lidídi shírat dódi lekármo / kérem hayáh lidídi
> beqéren ben shámen—*

My beloved has a vineyard
On a very fruitful hill.
He dug it up and cleared away its stones,
And planted it with the choicest vine.
He built a tower in its midst,
And also made a winepress in it. (Isaiah 5:1–2)

It is significant that Jesus begins by invoking images from this Isaian prophecy, because the parable of the vine growers does, in fact, explore Jesus' historical relationship to the prophets. Moreover, as we shall see, he tells his parable in a way that further interprets the poem of Isaiah.

As to the meaning of the "vineyard," the explanatory note in Isaiah left no doubt: "For the vineyard of the LORD of hosts *is* the house of Israel, / And the men of Judah are His pleasant plant" (5:7). The "vineyard" has the same meaning in Jesus' parable.

The vine or vineyard as a metaphor for Israel was fairly common. Referring to the Exodus and Israel's occupation of the Holy Land, Asaph the Seer had prayed,

You have brought a vine out of Egypt,
You have cast out the nations, and planted it.
You provided for it,
And caused it to take deep root,
And it filled the land. (Psalm 80:8–9)

To this twin theme of the Exodus and the Conquest, Isaiah added a reference to Jerusalem—"a very fruitful hill"—the city where Jesus' own parable was delivered. Both Isaiah's poem, then, and Jesus' parable are concerned with the history of Jerusalem, the appointed capital of God's people.

Second, Jesus' parable narrates the history of Israel in terms of God's expectations: "Now when vintage-time drew near, he sent his servants to the vinedressers, that they might receive its fruit" (Matthew 21:34). This feature of the vineyard, too, Jesus took from Isaiah, who declared that God "*expected* it to bring forth grapes" (5:2).

At this point, however, Jesus expands the story by summarizing a sequence in which God at various times dispatches the prophets to receive an accounting from Israel:

> Now when vintage-time drew near, he sent his servants to the vinedressers, that they might receive its fruit. And the vinedressers took his servants, beat one, killed one, and stoned another. Again he sent other servants, more than the first, and they did likewise to them. (Matthew 21:34–36)

This was not the only time Jesus recalled the dark and costly fate of the prophets. He elsewhere described his contemporaries as the "sons of those who murdered the prophets" (Matthew 23:31).

Third, the narrative arrives at its culminating point, which is the mission of the Son:

> Then the owner of the vineyard said, "What shall I do? I will send my beloved son. Probably they will respect him when they see him." (Luke 20:13)

In Luke, as in Mark (12:6), the son in the parable is described as "my beloved," *agapetos mou*, the same expression the Father used to address Jesus at both his baptism and his Transfiguration.[11]

This identical expression—*agapetos mou*—is found, likewise, in the Septuagint (Greek) version of Isaiah's poem—"*My beloved* has a vineyard." Here *agapetos mou* translates Isaiah's Hebrew expression *dódi*, "my beloved." Jesus' parable, then, identifies the son as the "my beloved" in Isaiah's poem. It is to *him* that the vineyard truly belongs because he is the heir. He is the son with regard to God, and the heir with regard to Israel's history.

Fourth, the vine growers cannot plead ignorance for their crime, because they recognize the son, and their very recognition of him fuels their malice:

> But when the vinedressers saw him, they reasoned among themselves, saying, "This is the heir. Come, let us kill him, that the inheritance may be ours." (Luke 20:14)

This, then, is Jesus' interpretation of both his mission and his coming death: he is the "heir" of the ancient ministry of the prophets. Because of this, says Jesus, the unfaithful vine growers "cast him out of the vineyard and killed him" (20:15). He sees that his own murder will be the culminating crime in Israel's continued rejection of God and his messengers.

The parable's identification of Jesus as Son and heir—the fulfillment of prophetic history—passed into Christian theology very early, as we see in the epistle to the Hebrews:

> God, who at various times and in various ways spoke in time past to the fathers by the *prophets*, has in these last days spoken to us by a *Son*, whom he has appointed *heir* of all things. (1:1–2, emphasis added)

Finally, it appears probable that this self-interpretation of Jesus had taken shape only gradually over the previous two years as he continued to reflect on the prophets in the light of his own experience, especially the growing antagonism of his enemies. Jesus finally expressed this understanding during the last week of his life, in this dramatic parable.

By that time, Jesus was aware of the finality of the hour; something truly new and revolutionary was soon to happen—to wit, Jerusalem would be destroyed, and the care of the vineyard would pass to a new stewardship:

Therefore what will the owner of the vineyard do to them? He
will come and destroy those vinedressers and give the vineyard
to others. (Luke 20:15–16)

Much of Jesus' preaching, during the final week of his life,
was taken up with the impending destruction of Jerusalem and
the other signs that would inaugurate the final stages of world
history.[12]

THE WIDOW AT THE TREASURY

Among the various precincts in the temple at Jerusalem, Jesus especially favored the Court of Women. Unlike the Court of Israel, this
section was open to all the Jews, so Jesus chose it as a normal venue
in which to teach.

Notable in this area were thirteen trumpet-shaped collection
boxes, into which the devout might cast their donations. Each of
these boxes bore an inscription specifying the use to which the
money, deposited in this particular box, would be put. Jesus sometimes taught near those receptacles (cf. John 8:20).

On a certain day early in the last week of his life, Jesus

looked up and saw the rich putting their gifts into the treasury,
and He saw also a certain poor widow putting in two mites. So
He said, "Amen, I say to you that this poor widow has put in
more than all; for all these out of their abundance have put in
offerings, but she out of her poverty put in all the livelihood that
she had." (Luke 21:1–4)

These two coins were so small that they had no equivalent in
Roman money. To his readers in Rome, therefore, Mark explained
that two of them were needed to equal a single *quadrans* ("quarter"),
the lowest unit of Roman coinage (Mark 12:42).

Jesus' reaction was typical of him; this was not the only occasion on which he took compassion on a widow (cf. Luke 7:11–17). Indeed, Jesus was obviously fond of an old story of a strikingly similar widow who likewise sacrificed her last resources to advance God's cause.[13] Jesus knew that if such a woman was reduced even to ten coins, the loss of a single one of them was a matter of considerable concern and industry (cf. Luke 15:8–10).

Whereas Luke says the widow contributed "all her livelihood," Mark's version reads, *holon ton bion*, "her whole *life*" (Mark 12:44, emphasis added). For this reason, it is significant that this story of the poor widow in the temple places her in the immediate context of Jesus' Passion.

In Mark this story is found at the end of five stories of conflict between Jesus and his enemies (Mark 11:27–12:40) and immediately prior to his final great discourse—which commences with a remark about the grandeur of the temple (13:1)!

In Luke this widow appears in the chapter before the Sanhedrin's plot to kill Jesus (Luke 21:1–4; 22:1–6). Giving her *all* for God, she serves as a symbol of Jesus himself, who will lay down his life (*bios*) to advance the Father's cause.

In both gospels, Jesus "sees" this woman, understands her plight, and recognizes her likeness to himself—all of this within days of his death.

THE SEDER

The early tradition of Jesus' church cherished a special narrative of those events that transpired on the night of his betrayal by Judas Iscariot:

> I received from the Lord that which I also delivered to you: that the Lord Jesus on the night in which he was betrayed . . . (1 Corinthians 11:23)

Paul then goes on to tell the story of the Last Supper, a rite the early Christians—obeying Jesus' injunction to "do this"—repeated each Sunday as the central service of their worship.[14] The telling of the story of the Last Supper was a common feature of that familiar weekly service. Local variations in the wording of the service apparently account for the slight differences we find among the New Testament authors when they describe the historical event.[15]

The Synoptic Gospels explicitly identify the original supper as the Passover meal, the Seder.[16] At that supper, all the Evangelists agree, Jesus quietly confronted his betrayer, who then left the supper and went out to make arrangements for the betrayal. John, arguably, described it best: "Having received the piece of bread, he then went out immediately. And it was night" (John 13:30).

All the Evangelists, likewise, record Jesus' prediction of Simon Peter's denial of him.

Other details of the supper are found among the four gospels: John describes how the Savior washed the feet of the disciples and spoke to them about service to one another (John 13:3–17). Luke also records his exhortation to mutual service in humility (Luke 22:24–27). Only Luke speaks of further instructions about the coming apostolic mission (22:35–38).

Matthew (26:30) and Mark (14:26) both mention the Hallel (Psalms 113–118), customarily chanted near the end of the Seder. One of the most significant lines of the Hallel is Psalm 116:12–13.

> What shall I render to the Lord
> For all His benefits toward me?
> I will take up the cup of salvation,
> And call upon the name of the Lord.

Jesus' resolve to drink "the cup of salvation" would be sorely tried during the hours immediately to come.[17]

THE FATHER

John's account of the supper differs greatly from the others, both in form and substance, its most notable feature being Jesus' long discourse and prayer. This material fills most of five chapters in John, making the supper scene longer than any earlier episode in that gospel.

Most significant, perhaps, about John's Last Supper discourse is Jesus' constant reference to "the Father." Even before he commenced the public ministry—while he was yet a boy—Jesus had asked his mother, "Did you not know that I must be about the things of *my Father*?" (Luke 2:49). This was the same Father further revealed in the Son's baptism and transfiguration. It was to vindicate the claims of this Father that Jesus purged the temple: "Take these things away! Do not make my Father's house a house of merchandise!" (John 2:16).

As opposition against him grew stronger, especially during the last year of his ministry, Jesus became progressively more conscious of what terrible things fidelity to the Father would soon entail. He spoke incessantly on his relationship to the Father: "I am not alone, but I am with the Father who sent me. . . . The Father who sent me bears witness of me. . . . I speak what I have seen with my Father. . . . I honor my Father. . . . It is my Father who honors me. . . . The works that I do in my Father's name, they bear witness of me."[18]

The will of the Father was related to Jesus' death for the sheep:

> As the Father knows me, even so I know the Father; and I lay down my life for the sheep. . . . Therefore my Father loves me, because I lay down my life that I may take it again. . . . This command I have received from my Father.[19]

The Father himself gave these sheep to Jesus, and he loves them, as he loves the Father:

> My sheep hear my voice, and I know them, and they follow me.
> And I give them eternal life, and they shall never perish; nei-
> ther shall anyone snatch them out of my hand. My Father, who
> has given them to me, is greater than all; and no one is able to
> snatch them out of my Father's hand. I and the Father are one.
> (John 10:27–30)

It is obvious that Jesus, during the supper, was completely preoccupied with the Father. When, at an early age, he had dedicated
his life to "the things of my Father," that dedication became the
foundation of everything he did. This zeal for God was now about
to consume him, and the flame of it became more intense as the
hour drew near:

> Now before the Feast of the Passover, when Jesus knew that
> his hour had come that he should depart from this world to the
> Father, having loved his own who were in the world, he loved
> them to the extreme. (John 13:1)

Jesus, knowing "that the Father had given all things into his
hands, and that he had come from God and was going to God" (John
13:3), could not stop speaking of the *Father*. This word is heard from
his lips twenty-one times in John 14, ten times in John 15, twelve
times in John 16, and, always in direct address, six times in John 17.

The prayer of Jesus in John 17—often called the high-priestly
prayer—is especially solemn. It is easily the longest recorded prayer
of Jesus and most clearly elaborates the truth John had declared at
the beginning of the fourth gospel:

> In the beginning was the Word, and the Word was with God,
> and the Word was God. He was in the beginning with God. . . .
> In Him was life, and the life was the light of men. (John 1:1–3)

After reciting this long prayer to the Father, Jesus "went out with his disciples over the Brook Kidron, where there was a garden, which he and his disciples entered" (John 18:1). There he had an appointment to keep.

———————————————————————— 10 —

THE GARDEN

THE NARRATIVE TRADITION OF THE EARLY CHURCH—
preserved especially in her liturgical practice—fixed the Savior's
sufferings and death in a determined sequence that became standard. This explains why all four gospels are in substantial harmony
regarding that sequence. The fixing of the narrative tradition also
explains why all the Evangelists begin the Passion story on "the
night he was betrayed" (1 Corinthians 11:23).

In each of the Gospels except John, the description of Judas's
betrayal is preceded by an account of Jesus' agonizing prayer in the
garden.[1] This scene is also described in Hebrews 5:7–8. We will
consider all four accounts.

The scene of Jesus praying in the garden, on the night before
his death, is among the most disturbing presentations among the
gospel narratives. Specifically, Jesus' immense sadness and personal distress seem much out of character with what the gospel
stories—up to this point—would lead the reader to expect. What
has become of the serenity and self-assurance that tells the leper, "I
will it; be cleansed" (Matthew 8:3)? Where now is the confidence
that announces to the centurion, "I will come and heal him" (8:7),

or commands the wind and sea, "Peace, be still" (Mark 4:39)? In short, the image of Jesus in the garden stands in stark contrast to the picture we have of him from all prior scenes in his life.

From very early times, pagans themselves were quick to notice in the agony what they took to be an inconsistency with Christian belief in the divinity of Christ. Late in the second century, when the critic Celsus wrote the first formal treatise against the Christian faith, he cited Jesus' fear and discomposure in the garden as evidence against the doctrine of his divinity. Celsus inquired, "Why does [Jesus] shriek and lament and pray to escape the fear of destruction, speaking thus: 'Father, if it is possible, let this cup pass from me'?" In truth, reasoned Celsus, if Jesus so "lamented" (*oduretai*) his coming death, he does not appear to have been especially brave, much less divine!

The Christian apologist Origen, refuting Celsus in the following century, responded that the gospel's critic failed to appreciate Jesus' complete acceptance of the Father's will in his coming death. His petition for deliverance—as desperate as it seemed to be—was immediately followed by the words, "Nevertheless, not my will, but Yours be done." This sentiment, Origen went on, demonstrated Jesus' "piety and greatness of soul," his "firmness," and his "willingness to suffer."[2]

Needless to say, all Christians are at one with Origen's response to the objections of Celsus.

THE WEAKNESS OF GOD

Christians should also consider, nonetheless, the force of that pagan's argument. Although the "malice" (*kakourgon*) of Celsus denied him access to the true and deeper meaning of the agony, we must give him credit for discerning in it the full measure of Jesus' humanity. Even as we reject that critic's conclusion, we are obliged to recognize its force.

That is to say, the fullness of Jesus' humanity was most manifest in the event described in the epistle to the Hebrews as "the days of his flesh" (5:7). In the Savior's agony, believers perceive the most profound and disturbing inferences of the doctrine of the Incarnation—the "enfleshing" of God's Son.

More than anywhere else in the New Testament, the garden scene presents us with the phenomenon of frailty and conflict in the mind and heart, as Jesus struggles with the trauma of his impending Passion. Indeed, he speaks of this conflict in terms of spirit and flesh. It is during—and with respect to—his experience in the garden that he declares, "The spirit indeed is willing, but the flesh is weak" (Matthew 26:41). To be *in the flesh* is to feel weak. He knew whereof he spoke!

Whether the conflict is portrayed in terms of sorrow (Matthew and Mark) or of fear (Luke and Hebrews), the New Testament sources agree that Jesus did not *want* to suffer and die this painful and most ignominious death, and he prayed to be delivered from it. Here, above all, we are presented with the profound mystery of self-emptying that the apostle Paul called "the weakness of God." Each account of the agony likewise demonstrates, nonetheless, how "the weakness of God is stronger than men" (1 Corinthians 1:25).

The inner conflict described in the New Testament was based on an opposition between the powerful psychological disposition of Jesus—his desire to live!—and what he perceived to be the will and call of God. The two options were mutually exclusive. Luke calls the experience a "struggle," an *agonia*.

In this scene, according to all four sources, Jesus' intense psychological experience of weakness and turmoil was followed by a determined resolution, which is perhaps the most significant element in the story. Jesus was clearly stronger and more serene when he left the garden, even though his captors had forcefully bound him.

In respect to this sense of resolution, it is instructive to contrast the turbulence and trauma of Jesus in the garden not only with earlier scenes in his life but also with his composure during the rest of the night and the following day.[3]

The epistle to the Hebrews tells of both Jesus' fear and his subsequent sense of assurance. Speaking of the first, it says that Jesus "offered up prayers and supplications, with vehement cries and tears to Him who was able to save him from death" (5:7). With reference to the second, it declares that Jesus, "for the joy that was set before him, endured the cross, despising the shame" (12:2).

Jesus' new composure and sense of resolution continued to the end. In the course of his two trials—Jewish and Roman—he maintained a demeanor both calm and self-possessed, even as he endured indignities and unbelievable suffering. Thus, his final statement to the Sanhedrin was both solemn and self-assured.[4] No less dignified and confident were his few pronouncements to Pilate,[5] and he honored Herod's curiosity with not a single syllable (Luke 23:9). In all these cases, Jesus acted with a dignity beyond his tormentors' reach.

This renewed strength, moreover, was conveyed to Jesus through his experience of prayer. According to all four accounts of the event, it was in prayer that Jesus resolved the conflict in his soul. In fact, each writer goes into some detail to describe this prayer and the transforming resolution to which it led.

We recognize, in short, that Jesus' prayer in the garden—his prayerful acquiescence in the Father's will—strengthened him for the dreadful ordeal to come. The Passion story testifies to the personally transforming power of this prayer. From the perspective of psychology, Jesus was a truly different person after this spiritual struggle.

THE WITNESSES

Although I propose to examine the four literary accounts of the agony with particular attention to their differences, we should begin by mentioning their common historical source in the testimony of the select individuals who directly witnessed the event: Peter, James, and John. These were the men who beheld Jesus, "who, in the days of his flesh, . . . offered up prayers and supplications, with vehement cries and tears to Him who was able to save him from death" (Hebrews 5:7).

Indeed, the reference to "vehement cries and tears" explains how the early believers came to know about this event—that is, from the apostles specifically named as being near the scene. All the accounts go back to these three men. As far as we can discern, they alone—situated only "a little farther" off (Matthew 26:39), "about a stone's throw" away (Luke 22:41)—were able to see Jesus' kneeling posture (Mark 14:35) and to hear those "vehement cries."

This was no scene for the timid, and Jesus' selection of these witnesses was surely related to other evidence of their eminence throughout the Gospels. It is reasonable to surmise that the Savior prepared the chosen witnesses by certain earlier experiences special to them. Thus, only Peter, James, and John were permitted entrance into the chamber where Jesus confronted and conquered the power of death in the person of Jairus's daughter.[6] These three, likewise, were the sole witnesses to Jesus' transfiguration on the mountain.[7]

Over the centuries, Christian homiletics and hymnography have copiously testified to a common Christian persuasion on this point: Peter, James, and John received these special revelations of Jesus' innate glory and his sovereign power over death, in order to be strengthened to endure the sight of his agony in the garden.

We do well to consider the element of "planning" in this matter because the preservation of this story was neither a decree of fate nor an accident of circumstances. It was entirely deliberate. Jesus could certainly have suffered this agony in solitary privacy, but he determined that there would be witnesses to it—close enough to behold the scene—because he wanted this scene to be recorded!

Jesus resolved that all his disciples—including "those who have not seen and yet have believed" (John 20:29)—should become familiar with him in that hour when he was most obviously human.

Having determined, then, on the choice of these three men to be witnesses, Jesus was careful to prepare their souls for the ordeal. He set them aside and took them with him on those specific occasions that would give them strength.

As for these witnesses, they hardly covered themselves with glory that night. In spite of the exhortation they received to "stay here and keep watch," they kept falling asleep. In fact, Jesus came to them three times to complain, "Could you not watch with me one hour?"[8]

It is important to reflect that we are acquainted with the failure of these apostles because *they* were the ones who testified to it. Their failure was part of the story, and they recognized it as such. Consequently, when they later narrated to others the events of that night, they made sure not to omit the account of Jesus' disappointment with them.

Indeed, they failed the Savior. Had Jesus seen the three of them steady at prayer, supporting him in his time of fear and sorrow, his spirit—like any human spirit at such a time—would have been strengthened. Thus, an added component of his trauma that night was the loss of human encouragement from those witnesses, who should have supplied it. He knew these men well enough, nonetheless. Earlier in the evening, had he not told them, "All of you will be tripped up tonight" (Matthew 26:31)?

LEARNING OBEDIENCE

We are now ready to look more closely at the individual literary accounts of that dreadful night, "the night he was betrayed." Having already cited the epistle to the Hebrews—which may be our earliest

written reference to the agony[9]—let us begin with this account. It is
the shortest, speaking only of

> Jesus, who, in the days of his flesh, when he had offered up
> prayers and supplications, with vehement cries and tears to Him
> who was able to save him from death, and was heard because of
> his godly fear, though he were a Son, yet he learned obedience by
> the things which he suffered. (Hebrews 5:7–8)

This terrible scene took place, says Hebrews, "in the days of
his flesh." The "flesh" here refers not to the Incarnation as such
(because the Word's assumption of our humanity is permanent, not
temporary), but to the condition of human weakness, which God's
Son willingly assumed so "that through death he might destroy him
who had the power of death, that is, the devil" (Hebrews 2:14).

This is a major argument in the epistle to the Hebrews. The
author of this work speaks of Jesus' death not just as an objective
and clinical fact but as a matter of *experience*; he employs the metaphor of *taste*. He writes,

> We see Jesus, who was made a little lower than the angels, for the
> suffering of death crowned with glory and honor, that he, by the
> grace of God, might *taste death* for every person. (Hebrews 2:9,
> emphasis added)

That is to say, Jesus conquered death not simply by dying but by
going through the experience—the *taste*—of dying.[10]

This was necessarily the case, the author of Hebrews argues,
because death is not only a human fact but also an abiding source of
human fear. The thought of death is man's companion throughout
life. It was this fear of death that Jesus faced in prayer:

Inasmuch then as the children have partaken of flesh and blood,
he himself likewise shared in the same, that through death he
might destroy him who had the power of death, that is, the devil,
and release those who *through fear of death* were all their lifetime
subject to bondage. (Hebrews 2:14–15, emphasis added)

According to Hebrews, then, God's Son assumed, not simply
human nature, but the existential burden of human experience. His
was to be a full and felt solidarity, in which "he is not ashamed to
call them brothers, saying: 'I will declare Your name to my brothers'" (Hebrews 2:11–12). For this reason, declares Hebrews, "in all
things he had to be made like the brothers" (2:17). These "all things"
particularly included the tasting of death.

The object of Jesus' "prayers and supplications," the author
goes on, was deliverance from death. This feature of his agony,
described in Hebrews, corresponds to the Gospel accounts in which
Jesus prays that he may be spared the "cup" of his coming sufferings (Matthew 26:39, 42) and that "the hour might pass from him"
(Mark 14:35).

Hebrews stresses the experiential aspect of this obedience to
the Father's will. Indeed, Jesus "learned obedience by the things
which He suffered," a parallel to the Gospel accounts in which the
Savior, in his agony, submits his own will obediently to that of his
Father.[11] Similarly, the apostle Paul preserves part of a hymn that
speaks of Jesus' obedience unto death, "even the death of the cross"
(Philippians 2:8).

This obedience of Jesus was not theoretical, detached, or
instantaneous. He *learned* it through the actual process of suffering and dying. Jesus was inwardly *changed* through this experience,
thereby becoming "perfected" (Hebrews 5:9). He was "made perfect
through sufferings" (2:10).

THE REVERENT PRIEST

In addition, says Hebrews, the prayers and supplications of Jesus were themselves sacrificial in that he "offered" them (*prosenegkas*). They were priestly prayers. That is to say, Jesus' sacrifice had even now begun here in the garden. His Passion is a seamless whole. Already we perceive in his prayers and supplications the true essence of sacrifice, which is the inner oblation of oneself to God.

The book of Hebrews insists, furthermore, that these "prayers and supplications" of Jesus were *heard* on high, precisely because of "his godly fear," which is to say his piety and reverence (*evlabeia* in Greek; *reverentia* in the Latin Vulgate). Jesus' obedient reverence is exactly what we find in the Gospel accounts of the agony.

In what sense, then, was Jesus "heard" when he offered these prayers and supplications?

To answer this question properly, it is useful to remember a principle of all godly petition—namely, "Now this is the confidence that we have in Him, that if we ask anything *according to His will*, He hears us" (1 John 5:14, emphasis added).

Jesus prayed explicitly *according to God's will*; indeed, it was the very essence of his prayer. Therefore, his prayer *was heard* according to God's will. He was not delivered from death in the sense that he avoided death, but in the sense that he conquered it, that he was victorious over death, that in his own death he trampled down death forever.

This is to say that Jesus' resurrection and glorification were the Father's response to his prayer in the agony. It was an answer to *this* prayer—"Thy will be done"—so that Jesus, "having been perfected, . . . became the author of eternal salvation to all who obey him" (Hebrews 5:9).

This *was* God's will, the will that Jesus prayed would be done. He was thus "made perfect through sufferings" (Hebrews 2:10). It was because the Savior became obedient unto death that "God also has highly exalted Him" (Philippians 2:9). The Paschal victory over death was the Father's reply to the prayers and supplications offered by the true High Priest in the days of his flesh.

OBEDIENCE AND THE BODY

According to Hebrews, Jesus subjected to the Father not only the assent of his will but also the disposition of his flesh. In this regard, the author of Hebrews places on the lips of the Son, "when he came into the world," the words of the psalmist,

> Sacrifice and offering You did not desire,
> But a body You have prepared for me.
> In burnt offerings and sacrifices for sin You had no pleasure.
> Then I said, "Behold, I have come—in the volume of the
> book it is written of me—to do Your will, O God."
> (Hebrews 10:5–7; Psalm 40:6–8)

"*A body* You have prepared for me," says the incarnate Word to his Father. We may contrast the Greek text of Hebrews here to the Hebrew text of Psalm 40:6, which reads, "Sacrifice and offering You did not desire; *my ears* You have opened." It appears that the author of Hebrews, perhaps relying on the Septuagint (as reflected in its three earliest extant manuscripts), preferred "body" to "ears." He thereby asserted that Jesus *in his very body*—and not simply in the assent of his will—accomplished our redemption. In his prayer in the garden, Jesus handed over not only his will but also his flesh.

Some Christians have imagined that human redemption was wrought not on Golgotha but in Gethsemane, at the hour when Jesus explicitly submitted his will in obedience to the will of the

Father. They proposed the theory that our redemption was purchased not by the immolation of Jesus' body on the cross but by his internal, spiritual sufferings in the garden.

According to this view, redemption was accomplished by the deliberate submission of Jesus' human will to the divine will. Indeed, some have endeavored to bolster this thesis through the biblical principle that the true sacrifice acceptable to God consists in an internal immolation of the heart:

> For You do not desire sacrifice, or else I would give it;
> You do not delight in burnt offering.
> The sacrifices of God are a broken spirit,
> A broken and a contrite heart—
> These, O God, You will not despise. (Psalm 51:16–17)

I do not believe this theory corresponds to the teaching of the epistle to the Hebrews, according to which "we have been sanctified through the offering of *the body* of Jesus Christ" (Hebrews 10:10, emphasis added). A full Christian view of redemption will insist that it takes place *in the body*. To separate the suffering and death of Christ *in the flesh* from the internal submission of his will to the Father, in my opinion, does violence to the Holy Scriptures.

Indeed, such thinking does violence to the Incarnation itself, whereby

> He himself likewise shared in [flesh and blood] that *through death* he might destroy him who had the power of death, that is, the devil. (Hebrews 2:14, emphasis added)

Jesus paid the price of man's sins not simply by accepting death but by the actual human experience of dying—by *tasting death*.

Thus, the submission of Jesus' will led directly to the immolation of his body and the libation of his blood. His agony in the garden pertained to a single purpose, extending from the Word's assumption of our flesh all the way to his ascent into heaven. The Christian faith knows of no redemption apart from what God's Son accomplished *in the flesh.*

MAN OF SORROWS

Interpreting the death and resurrection of Jesus in the light of earlier biblical literature, the first Christians savored the contrast between disobedient Adam and the obedient Christ, observing that

> as by one man's disobedience many were made sinners, so also by one Man's obedience many will be made righteous. (Romans 5:19; cf. 1 Corinthians 15:3–4)

The early believers easily perceived that whereas the first man attempted, in rebellion, to become God's equal, the second,

> being in the form of God, did not regard being equal to God a usurpation [*harpagmos*], but he emptied himself, taking the form of a bondservant, being made in the likeness of men, and being found in shape as a man, he humbled himself, becoming obedient unto death. (Philippians 2:6–8)

It is important to bear in mind the traditional contrast between the obedient Jesus and the disobedient Adam when we come to the Gospel accounts of the Savior's struggle at "Gethsemani."[12] The very name of this place means "olive garden," abbreviated to simply "a garden" by John (18:1).

If the epistle to the Hebrews stresses Jesus' encounter with fear, Matthew and Mark emphasize his experience of sadness. For them, this garden of Jesus' trial was, first of all, a place of sadness, the sorrow of death itself. "My soul is exceedingly sorrowful," said he, "even unto death."[13] Once again, we detect the parallel with Adam. This "sorrow unto death" is common to the two gardens of man's trial: Eden and Gethsemane.

In the garden of disobedience, the Lord spoke to Adam of his coming death, whereby he would return to the dust from which he was taken. Adam's curse introduced man's sadness unto death. Thus, in the Septuagint (Greek) version of this story, the Lord tells Eve, "I will greatly multiply your sorrows [lypas]," and "in sorrows [en lypais] you will bear your children." And to her husband the Lord declares, "Cursed is the ground for your sake; in sorrows [en lypais] you shall eat of it all the days of your life" (Genesis 3:16, 17).

In the light of this text, Matthew's and Mark's accounts of Jesus' obedience in the garden emphasize his sadness: "My soul is exceedingly sorrowful [perilypos], even unto death." The context of this assertion indicates that Jesus assumed the primeval curse of man's sorrow unto death, in order to reverse Adam's disobedience. In the garden he bore our sadness unto death, becoming the "Man of sorrows, and acquainted with grief" (Isaiah 53:3).

In the late fourth century, Ambrose of Milan, commenting on the agony in the garden, wrote of Jesus:

Nowhere do I wonder more at his piety and majesty, because it would have profited me less if he had not assumed my own feelings [affectum]. Therefore, the One that had no reason to sorrow for himself sorrowed for me, and leaving aside the enjoyment of his eternal divinity he is afflicted with the weariness of my infirmity. He assumed my sadness [tristitiam meam], in order to confer on me his joy, and in our footsteps he descended even to the sorrow of death [ad mortis aerumnam], in order to recall us to life in his own footsteps.[14]

In the garden Jesus returns to the very place of Adam's fall, taking upon himself Adam's sorrow unto death. Thus, Ambrose regards Christ's assumption of man's sadness in the garden as integral to the Incarnation. He comments,

> Therefore, I confidently use the word "sadness," because I preach the Cross—because he did not assume the appearance of the Incarnation, but its truth. Consequently, he had to assume grief (*dolorem suscipere*), in order to overcome sadness (*tristitiam*), not to avoid it.[15]

THE FATHER'S WILL

When he addresses God in the garden, Jesus addresses him as *Abba*, the affectionate and more familiar vocative form of "Father" in Aramaic (Mark 14:36).[16] In fact, Jesus always addresses God as "Father," except in the one place where he prays words from the Psalter.[17]

In this Father he has total confidence, telling Peter in the garden, "Or do you think that I cannot now pray to my Father, and He will provide me with more than twelve legions of angels?" (Matthew 26:53).

As he confronts the enemies who will, in due course, see to his murder, Jesus speaks of a strong sense of being "with" the Father. He tells them, "I am not alone, but I am with the Father who sent me" (John 8:16). Again, "He who sent me is with me. The Father has not left me alone, for I always do those things that please Him" (8:29). And again, this time to the disciples: "I am not alone, because the Father is with me" (16:32).

Jesus does not hold back from his Father the natural repugnance he feels at what lies immediately ahead. He is a true man, fully human; can we expect anything less? This repugnance—fear, sadness, and deep disappointment—must be worked through in the process of his prayer. Even as he submits to the Father's will, he must tell the Father exactly what he feels:

Abba, Father, all things are possible for You. Take this cup away from me; nevertheless, not what I will, but what You will. (Mark 14:36)

This final phrase embodies, in fact, the way Jesus taught his disciples to pray. Even as they asked for their daily bread and deliverance from evil, they were to say, "Thy will be done."

This petition—"Thy will be done"—does not represent a hypothesis or a limitation laid on the prayer. "What You will" is not a restriction of Jesus' confidence but an elevation of it. It expresses a constitutive feature of his prayer and an essential component of his faith.

The real purpose of the Son's prayer, after all, is not to inform the Father what he wants but to hand himself over more completely, in faith, to what the Father wants. The purpose of all prayer, even the prayer of petition, is living communion with God. The man who tells the Father, then, "Thy will be done," does not thereby show himself a weaker believer but a stronger one. Jesus, "the author and perfecter of our faith," models this prayer. He gives his disciples, in this form, the very essence of true prayer.

The "will of God," in which Jesus places the trust of his petition, is not a blind, arbitrary, or predetermined will. It is, rather, the abiding love of the Father. This theology of prayer is conveyed in Jesus' prayer in the garden, by which his own human will is obediently united with the will of God.

THE ANGEL AND THE BLOOD

We come now to the gospel of Luke, from whom we gain the very term "agony" to describe Jesus' ordeal in the garden (Luke 22:44). He is the only New Testament writer to use this word.

Luke omits the threefold form of Jesus' prayer found in Mark and Matthew. His version, therefore, is shorter. It does contain, however, certain particulars not found in the other accounts of the drama in the garden.[18]

The traditional form of the Lukan text says,

> Then an angel appeared to him from heaven, strengthening him. And being in agony, he prayed more earnestly. Then his sweat became like great drops of blood falling down to the ground. (Luke 22:43–44)

These particulars about the bloody sweat and the comforting angel we know only from Luke. Let us consider them more closely.

First, the sweat of blood is a condition called *hematidrosis*. This pathology, which results from an extreme dilation of the subcutaneous capillaries, causes them to burst through the sweat glands. This symptom, mentioned as early as Aristotle,[19] is well-known to the history of medicine, which sometimes associates it with intense fear. It is not without interest, surely, that Luke, the only Evangelist to mention this phenomenon, was a physician.

Unlike Mark (14:34) and Matthew (26:38), Luke does not speak of Jesus' sadness in the garden scene, but of an inner struggle, an *agonia*, in which the Savior "prayed more earnestly."

The theological significance of this feature in Luke is that Jesus' internal conflict causes the first bloodshed in the Passion. His complete obedience to the Father in his prayer immediately produces this initial libation of his redemptive blood, the blood of which he had proclaimed just shortly before, "This cup is the new covenant in my blood, which is shed for you" (Luke 22:20).

Prior to the appearance of his betrayer, then, Jesus already begins the shedding of his blood. He pours it out in the struggle of obedience, before a single hand has been laid upon him. In Luke's account the agony in the garden is not a prelude to the Passion but its very commencement, because Jesus' stern determination to accomplish the Father's will causes his blood to flow—already—as the price for man's redemption.

Second, an angel is sent to strengthen Jesus during his trial. Luke, in his earlier temptation scene, had omitted the angelic ministry, of which Matthew (4:11) and Mark (1:13) spoke on that occasion. When Luke did describe that period of temptation, however, he remarked that the demon, having failed to bring about Jesus' downfall, "departed from him *until an opportune time*" (4:13, emphasis added). Now, in the garden, that *time* has come, and Jesus receives the ministry of an angel to strengthen him for the task.

In Luke's literary structure, this ministering "angel of the agony" stands parallel to Gabriel at the beginning of the gospel. In the earlier case an angel introduces the Incarnation; in the present case an angel introduces the Passion. Very shortly angels will introduce the Resurrection (Luke 24:4).

THE KISS

It was some time after midnight when the armed band left the house of Caiaphas, well to the south of the temple, proceeded northward along the Brook Kidron, and approached the little bridge by which they could cross over to the Mount of Olives on the eastern side. Those in the front carried lanterns and flambeaus to light the way, for the night was dark in spite of the full moon of Passover. Some of the band were armed with swords, while others carried only clubs (Matthew 26:47). Attaining the eastern side, the group veered north again to the olive garden, situated on the side of the mount.

Judas Iscariot, "the son of perdition" (John 17:12), a defector from the small group of Jesus' close companions, guided this band, for he was the one who could, in the relative darkness, identify Jesus from within the number of people present.

Jesus was ready for this, of course. Even as early as the previous Passover (John 6:4)—a year ago—Jesus had spoken of this coming betrayal:

> Jesus answered them, "Did I not choose you, the twelve, and one of you is a devil?" He spoke of Judas Iscariot, the son of Simon, for it was he who would betray him, being one of the twelve. (John 6:70–71)

It is not clear just how Judas began the downward path that would lead him, in due course, to such an act so treacherous that Jesus said of him,

> Woe to that man by whom the Son of Man is betrayed! It would have been better for that man if he had not been born. (Matthew 26:24)

We are given some hint, nonetheless, that the root of Judas's problem was plain and simple avarice. According to the Evangelist John, when the betrayer complained about the "waste" of the ointment poured on Jesus just a few days earlier,

> he said this, not that he cared for the poor, but because he was a thief, and had the money box; and he used to take what was put in it. (John 12:6)

The bargain with the Sanhedrin was struck on Wednesday of that week, when

> one of the twelve, called Judas Iscariot, went to the chief priests and said, "What are you willing to give me if I deliver him to you?" And they counted out to him thirty pieces of silver. So

from that time he sought opportunity to betray him. (Matthew
26:14–16)

Jesus knew, of course, exactly what was going on during those
previous several days. He was well aware that "Satan entered Judas,
surnamed Iscariot, who was numbered among the twelve" (Luke
22:3). Jesus also knew that the night in the garden was the night of
the betrayal. During the Seder, just a few hours before the appearance of this band of soldiers, he had instructed Judas, "What you
do, do quickly" (John 13:27).

Now the betrayer arrives, "guide to those who arrested Jesus"
(Acts 1:16), and says to the Master, "*Shalom*, Rabbi" (Matthew
26:49). The giveaway sign is an easy one: Judas simply walks up to
Jesus and kisses his hand, the customary greeting a disciple gave to
his rabbi as a mark of affectionate respect.

In greeting his betrayer, Jesus draws attention to the awful
irony of the act: "Judas, are you betraying the Son of Man with a
kiss?" (Luke 22:48). According to Matthew (26:50), Jesus addresses
Judas here as "friend."

In Mark's account, there is yet another witness to the event:

Now a certain young man followed him, having a linen cloth
thrown around his naked body. And the young men laid hold
of him, and he left the linen cloth and fled from them naked.
(Mark 14:51–52)

There is considerable merit in the view that that young man
was the author of this gospel, Mark himself. Not much older than
a boy at the time, Mark was the son of a woman named Mary, in
whose home the earliest Christians in Jerusalem were accustomed
to meet for their common worship (Acts 12:12).

THE SEVERED EAR

It is unlikely that Simon Peter and Malchus knew each other, the one being a fisherman in Galilee and the other a servant of the high priest in Jerusalem. Nor was it probable, in the normal course of affairs, that their paths would ever cross. Destiny, however, brought them together in the garden that night because Malchus was part of the armed band sent by the high priest to arrest Jesus.

There is no reason to believe that Malchus himself regarded the coming event as especially significant. It had nothing to do with him, after all; he was simply the faithful servant of the high priest, expected to perform this task loyally, leaving to his betters the determination of such difficult matters.

Simon Peter—to return to the sequence of our story—was once again awakened by Jesus, having fallen asleep three times in as many hours, even as he listened to Jesus' prayer. Weak in flesh, Simon had utterly failed in the Master's command to watch and pray with him (Matthew 26:41).

For Simon Peter, what a night! At the Passover Seder, just a few hours before, Jesus had disclosed the presence of a traitor among them and foretold that the rest of the little group would fail him in his coming hour of trial (Matthew 26:21–24, 31). Simon himself had been singled out for a special warning, as the Lord predicted his triple denial before that very night should run its course (26:33–35). It was all entirely too much for a man to bear, so Simon had slept there on the ground, under the olive trees.

But now he was awakened by the Lord's voice: "Rise, let us be going. See, my betrayer is at hand" (Matthew 26:46). And here they were, a band of armed men already on the scene. Simon leapt up, holding a sword that he had brought along to make good his promise of loyalty in the face of danger. He recognized Judas Iscariot, who came forward and kissed the hand of his rabbi. Just what was this all about?

Jesus' response explained it all: "Judas, are you betraying the Son of Man with a kiss?" (Luke 22:48).

Simon waited no further.

In the reflected glare of the torches, Malchus saw the flashing sword coming at him swiftly from the right—apparently a backhand swing aimed at his throat—and he ducked to his left to avoid decapitation. Even so, the blow glanced along his helmet so that his right ear was partly severed by the tip of the blade (Luke 22:50). Just then, however, Jesus stepped forward, grabbed the dangling ear, and calmly replaced it on the head of the high priest's servant, as though the thing had never happened.

For Malchus, the rest of that night was a blur and the whole next day, as he walked around in a daze, going to Pilate's palace and elsewhere but reaching up, from time to time, to feel his ear and trying to make sense of it all.

Some decades later, Malchus—a Christian now for many years and long repentant of his actions on that dreadful night—sat down and described his part in the event to a physician named Luke, who happened to be writing a new account of the ministry and teaching of Jesus. Malchus told how the Savior reached out his hand through the enveloping darkness and reattached the dangling ear. Malchus asked Luke not to include his name in the account, unaware that another writer would put it in anyway (John 18:10).

This other writer, John, had also been present when it happened, and he may have learned Malchus's name from a cousin who encountered Simon in the courtyard of the high priest somewhat later that night (John 18:26).

As for Peter, he reluctantly followed Jesus' directive to put away the sword. This was the last time Peter was to show much courage that night.

11

THE BRIDEGROOM IS TAKEN AWAY

JESUS, AFTER HIS ARREST IN THE GARDEN, WAS TAKEN TO the house of the high priest, to be tried before the Sanhedrin, Judaism's high court. After this body failed to convict him on the strength of false testimony, Jesus was found guilty of blasphemy. The high priest had asked him, "Are you the Christ, the Son of the Blessed?" That is, Jesus was asked to admit to his claim that he was God's Son. To this he answered, "I am. And you will see the Son of Man sitting at the right hand of the Power, and coming with the clouds of heaven" (Mark 14:61–62).

In the morning, Jesus was taken to the Roman procurator, Pontius Pilate, who was obliged to adjudicate the death sentence imposed by the Sanhedrin. At Jesus' hearing before Pilate, not one syllable was said about blasphemy. Instead, Jesus was accused of fomenting sedition against the Roman government. At one point in the hearing, his accusers let slip the fact that the complaint against Jesus was—in all truth—theological and religious: "We have a Law, and according to the Law he ought to die, because he made himself the Son of God" (John 19:7).

Whatever this claim meant to Pilate, "he was the more afraid."

169

In the end, the charge of sedition is what stuck: "If you let this man go, you are not Caesar's friend. Whoever makes himself a king speaks against Caesar" (19:12). Thus, Jesus was condemned to death by the two best legal systems of the time, the Jewish and the Roman.

The process of his trial and execution brought out both the best and worst of the people involved. Let us consider Jesus' final hours through the eyes of some of them.

PETER'S DENIALS

Among the Savior's deepest disappointments, even during the course of his trial before the Sanhedrin, was Simon Peter's three-fold denial of even knowing him. Peter's prominence and leadership among the disciples rendered this denial especially painful.

Unlike Peter's attempt to walk on water—recorded only in Matthew (14:28–33)—his denials of Jesus are chronicled in all four gospel accounts. Essentially the same in outline, the four versions of the story differ in certain details, some subtle, some indicating perspectives peculiar to an individual Evangelist.

Only John, for example, breaks up the sequence of the denials, mixing them into other features of the Passion account instead of telling them all at once. Thus, after Peter's first denial (John 18:17), the narrator leaves Peter and returns to Jesus' interrogation by Annas (18:19–23). Then, when Jesus is sent to Caiaphas (18:24), the narrator goes back to Peter and continues with the next two denials.

In this way, the structure of John's account is able to advance the story line in two different settings simultaneously—the courtroom and the outer hall—each setting enhancing the drama of the other. This style of narrative is also John's way of indicating that Peter's denials were spread over several hours.

Moreover, John alone mentions the charcoal fire, an element that ties the story of Peter's denials to the postresurrection account of his triple protestation of love for Jesus (John 18:18; 21:9). Both scenes contain the charcoal fire—*anthrakia*, a word not otherwise found in the New Testament. Thus, Peter's three denials are balanced by his threefold assertion of love for Jesus.

Mark, for his part, is alone among the Evangelists in including the detail that the rooster crowed *twice* (Mark 14:30, 68, 72). In fact, the first and second cockcrows refer to two different times during the night, hours apart, the second one around dawn. This is Mark's way of making the same point as John: Peter's was not a momentary lapse, but a sustained and repeated offense.

In general format, Matthew follows Mark's sequence of Peter's denials: Sitting outside the high priest's residence, in the courtyard, Peter is approached by a servant maid (*paidiske*), who believes she recognizes him as a companion of Jesus. Peter stands accused here of only one thing—being "with" (*meta*) Jesus, a charge that Matthew is at pains to sustain by his constant references to Peter's being *with* Jesus all through this chapter.[1]

Surrounded by a crowd, Peter denies the allegation in a voice loud enough to be heard by everybody (Matthew 26:70). Matthew adds this detail to Mark's version of the story (Mark 14:68), thus heightening the sense of Peter's fear and agitation. The insecure and bewildered disciple begins to move away—from the courtyard, to the porch, to the gate, finally outside.

The more Peter protests his unfamiliarity with Jesus, the more occasions he provides for the bystanders to detect the Galilean inflections in his speech: "Surely you also are one of them, for your speech betrays you" (Matthew 26:73). Thus, Peter is driven to greater desperation and begins to completely lose control.

The evidence of this breakdown is found in Peter's recourse to an oath in the second denial and to a curse in the third: "But again he denied with an oath, 'I do not know the man!' . . . Then he began to curse and swear, 'I do not know the man!'" (Matthew 26:72, 74).

The third denial is prompted by a more general accusation from "those who stood by" (Matthew 26:73). Several individuals make this accusation, and John's version of the story (John 18:26) includes among the crowd a relative of the man whose ear Peter wounded with a sword. This man, present at the arrest, now recognizes Peter.

Immediately after Peter's third denial, the rooster crows, prompting the apostle to remember what Jesus predicted. He remembers, leaves the place, and breaks into tears, now aware that he has added his own failure to the tragedy of the night: "So he went out and wept bitterly" (Matthew 26:75).

Luke's account of the episode lays a more explicit and poignant stress on Jesus' personal relationship with Peter.

To begin with, Luke includes a further detail about Jesus' prayer. We know that the Savior prayed for all the disciples that night (John 17:9), but Luke specifies that he prayed for Peter in a specific way, foreseeing Peter's defection. During the Seder, Jesus said to Peter:

> Simon, Simon! Indeed, Satan has asked for you, that he may sift you as wheat. But I have prayed for you, that your faith should not fail; and when you have returned, strengthen your brethren. (Luke 22:31–32)

We should make two remarks on this text:

First, Jesus likens his disciples to Job, telling them, "*Satan* has asked for *you* [plural]." These disciples, like Job, are going to be tempted by *Satan* that night. It is as though God spoke to *Satan* concerning each of the disciples, "Behold, all that he has is in your *power*" (Job 1:12). The "sifting" or shaking (*siniazo*), to which Satan will subject them, is a metaphor for the endurance of a trial. They will all experience the "scandal" of the cross.[2]

Second, Jesus' prayer is made for Peter specifically, so that the disciple's later conversion, when it comes, should strengthen the others. When Jesus tells Peter, "I have prayed for *you*, that *your* faith should not fail," it is important to observe that the "you" and "your"—in the canonical Greek text—are both singular in number. That is to say, Satan would sift *all* of them; however, Jesus prayed for *Peter*, in order that his later testimony will strengthen all of them.

Indeed, the story of Peter's denials has been a source of strengthening for Christian disciples down through the centuries.

Luke narrates another and more dramatic detail about Peter's three denials: Jesus turns and looks at the fallen apostle, just as the rooster crows. Luke describes it:

> Peter said, "Man, I do not know what you are saying!" Immediately, while he was still speaking, the rooster crowed. And the Lord turned and looked at Peter. Then Peter remembered the word of the Lord, how he had said to him, "Before the rooster crows, you will deny me three times." (Luke 22:60–61)

Thus, Peter's conscience receives the testimony of two senses—sight and hearing—as he simultaneously calls to mind the Savior's prophecy of his failure. His repentance is immediate: "So Peter went out and wept bitterly" (Luke 22:62).

PILATE'S WIFE

Since the story of Pilate's wife is found only in the gospel of Matthew (27:19), it seems reasonable to examine it specifically through the perspective of Matthew's story as a whole. What function does that very short narrative about Pilate's wife serve in that particular gospel?

Commentators have remarked that Pilate's wife, a Gentile woman who pleads the innocence of Jesus ("that just man"), serves as a foil to the Jewish leaders who clamor for his crucifixion (Matthew 27:23). This comment is surely accurate, but it does not indicate a larger context nor an intention specific to Matthew.

A closer examination of Matthew 27:19 is required. The text says that while Pilate

> was sitting on the judgment seat, his wife sent to him, saying, "Have nothing to do with that just man, for I have suffered many things today in a dream because of him."

This woman is portrayed not only as resistant to the official plot to murder Jesus but also as having "suffered many things today in a dream because of him." The most striking item here, I suggest, is her *dream*. It is with the dream that we should start.

This dream of a Gentile, coming near the end of Matthew's story, forms a literary inclusion with the dream of certain other Gentiles near that gospel's beginning. Most of Matthew's gospel fits between these dreams. With respect to those earlier dreamers, we were told, "being divinely warned *in a dream* that they should not return to Herod, they departed for their own country another way" (Matthew 2:12, emphasis added). That is the last appearance of the Magi.

The contexts of these two dreams—of the Magi and of Pilate's wife—are strikingly similar. In each case the dream takes place in connection with an official plot to murder Jesus. In the instance of the Magi, the plot includes the official representative of the Roman government, King Herod, who has "gathered all the chief priests and scribes of the people together" (Matthew 2:4). In the instance of Pilate's wife, the murderous plot involves "all the chief priests and elders of the people" (Matthew 27:1, 12, 20; the scribes are included in 27:41). In both cases the dreams of the Gentiles are contrasted with the plots of Jesus' enemies. Pilate's wife near the end of the story corresponds to the Magi near its beginning.

In each case, moreover, the plot to murder Jesus has to do with his kingship, his identity as the Messiah. In the example of the Magi, these travelers come from the east "to Jerusalem, saying, 'Where is he who has been born *King of the Jews?*'" (Matthew 2:1–2, emphasis added). The usurping Herod, threatened by the suspected appearance of Israel's true king, takes all the necessary precautions, including the murder of "all the male children who were in Bethlehem and in all its districts, from two years old and under" (2:16).

The expression "King of the Jews" does not appear in Matthew's story again until the final plot against Jesus. It is while Pilate officiates in his judgment seat, and just before receiving the message from his wife, that he inquires of Jesus, "Are you the King *of the Jews?*" (27:11). The source of Pilate's question here is indicated in the next verse, which tells us that "He was being accused by the chief priests and elders" (27:12). These chief priests and others correspond to the very group that Herod summoned earlier when he made his own inquiry about the King of the Jews.

Matthew tells us that Pilate "knew that they had handed him over because of envy." Indeed, Matthew mentions this detail in the verse immediately preceding the message from his wife (Matthew 27:18–19). This envy of Jesus' enemies readily puts the reader in mind of the earlier account of Herod's envy, when he was confronted with the real King of the Jews.

There is a special irony, then, in the title by which Pilate's soldiers address Jesus in their mockery: "Hail, *King of the Jews*" (27:29, emphasis added). Pilate, moreover, apparently with a view to mocking the Jews themselves, attaches to the cross the official accusation against Jesus: "This is Jesus, the *King of the Jews*" (27:37, emphasis added).

At last, then, is answered that question first advanced by the Magi, "Where is he who has been born King of the Jews?" (2:2). Now we know where he is because he hangs under a sign that announces to the entire world, "the King of the Jews."

Thus, the dream of Pilate's wife, which had revealed Jesus to be a just man, completes the earlier dream of the Magi. The testimony from the east is matched by the testimony from the West, both cases representing those regarding whom the risen Jesus will command his church, "Go therefore and make disciples of all nations" (28:19).

SCOURGED AND MOCKED

Once Pilate hands Jesus over for death, all discussion stops, and the tragedy starts to run its course. Indeed, it runs so quickly that details of enormous significance are barely mentioned.

For example, Mark (15:15) and Matthew (27:26) reduce the scourging of Jesus to a single participle—"having scourged Jesus," phragellosas. The Evangelists knew what this expression meant, as did their first readers, but clearly they were not disposed to elaborate the subject. Did they find Jesus' sufferings—his scourging in particular—too distressing to dwell on?

One suspects this was the case. In addition to the participle used by Mark and Matthew, all four gospels use another verb, mastigo, to tell of the Savior's scourging; they use this verb six times.[3] Eight times in all, then, the Evangelists speak of Jesus' scourging, always briefly and with restraint, avoiding the painful details. These would be too much for the reader to bear.

In this respect we may contrast the Evangelists with David and Isaiah. The Psalter and the book of Isaiah dwell lovingly on every wound in the Savior's body. The Old Testament accounts of Jesus' Passion are vivid and detailed; his very bones are numbered. Unlike the four Evangelists, these Old Testament prophets saw the Passion from a greater distance, so to speak, but they described it in greater detail. The four gospels, on the other hand, were closer to the event. When they were written, those sacred wounds were still very fresh in the minds of Christians. To many Christians, those wounds were simply unbearable to think about.

After all, the Evangelists and their first readers knew exactly what was entailed in those brief references to the scourging, especially when that form of torture accompanied a death sentence. In that setting there were no limits to the number of strokes or the ingenuity of the soldiers to inflict more pain and greater damage. Sometimes the beatings were so severe that the prisoners did not survive them. Indeed, the copious bleeding served to hasten a death on the cross. In this respect, we observe that the Savior's two crucified companions outlived him, and a strong case can be made that the immediate cause of Jesus' death was exsanguination.

If the four Evangelists were reluctant to describe the Savior's scourging in detail, however, they showed no corresponding disinclination to describe his mockery by the soldiers. In Mark, Matthew, and John this mockery particularly addressed Jesus' claims to kingship; as we saw, he was mocked as "King of the Jews."

In the use of this epithet, we should think of something close to "King of the Fools" in a medieval play. We should see in it the contempt those Gentiles felt toward Jews generally, a contempt they were eager to pour out on this particular Jew, whose own people abandoned him. Pilate expressed this same contempt by the inscription he caused to be affixed over Jesus' head on the cross. Suffering specifically as a Jew, Jesus became the supreme victim of anti-Semitism.

Jesus' true claim to the Davidic kingship renders the mockery scene supremely ironic. The mocking soldiers do, in fact, bend their knees before the King. Their salutation of him is—as the Evangelists and their readers know—theologically correct! Jesus is the same man who just days before, as he entered Jerusalem in triumph, was addressed as David's son.

In this mockery Jesus is clothed in a scarlet or purple garment— likely a military cloak—to mimic royalty. To adorn his head, the soldiers weave a crown of thorns, which serves as both a form of torture and a point of shame.

The theological significance of this crown of thorns comes from the Evangelists' understanding of it, not the intent of the mocking soldiers. The gospel writers knew, as do their readers in all ages, that the crown of Jesus was woven from the elements of Adam's curse: "Both thorns and thistles [the ground] shall bring forth for you" (Genesis 3:18). Jesus, wearing that crown, bears that curse.

According to John (19:5), Jesus is still wearing the robe and the thorny crown when he appears before the crowd, and he wears them still as that crowd shouts, "Crucify him!" Although the robe is removed after the mockery (Matthew 27:31), no Evangelist says that the crown is taken off. Christian art and hymnography commonly portray the crucified Christ as continuing to wear that crown on the cross, under the sign identifying him as "King of the Jews."

THE REVILING BENEATH THE CROSS

Matthew's description of the Crucifixion is the most detailed with respect to the mockery and reviling that Jesus endured:

And those who passed by blasphemed him, wagging their heads and saying, "You who destroy the temple and build it in three days, save yourself! If you are the Son of God, come down from the cross." Likewise the chief priests also, mocking with the scribes and elders, said, "He saved others; Himself he cannot save. If he is the King of Israel, let him now come down from the cross, and we will believe him. He trusted in God; let him deliver him now if He will have him; for he said, 'I am the Son of God.'" (Matthew 27:39–43)

This mockery, most elaborated by Matthew, is best understood in the general context of that gospel. Several reflections are in order.

First, in accepting this treatment without complaint or return of insult, Jesus exemplifies his own instructions in the Sermon on the Mount (Matthew 5–7). This patience extends Matthew's theme of a correspondence between that sermon and the mystery of the cross. In his sufferings, Jesus provided the concrete application of the sermon.

Second, following Mark (15:29), Matthew (27:39) understands this mockery of Jesus as "blasphemy." There is an irony in this indictment of blasphemy against Jesus' enemies here because this was the very charge that they had brought against him (Matthew 9:3; 26:65).

This understanding of the mockery as "blasphemy" presupposes, of course, the Christian confession of faith, according to which Jesus is the Son of God (Matthew 16:16). Because the title "Son of God" was the barbed point sticking in his enemies' craw (26:63), it appears also in the final taunts thrown at him (27:40, 43). This fact highlights the significance of the confession made by the presiding centurion at the moment of Jesus' death: "Truly this *was* the Son of God!" (27:54, emphasis added).

Third, the challenge, "*if* You are the Son of God," ties the story of the Crucifixion to Jesus' initial temptation, when Satan said to him, "*If* You are the Son of God . . ." (Matthew 4:3, 6). We recall that Satan issued that challenge just three verses after the Father's voice had proclaimed of Jesus, "This is My beloved Son" (3:17).

Thus, Matthew's great divide is between those who, with Simon Peter and the centurion, confess Jesus to be the Son of God and those who in satanic blasphemy deride this title. "Son of God" is the essential, defining confession.[4]

Fourth, Matthew's blasphemers, taunting Jesus to demonstrate his divine sonship by coming down from the cross, repeat the temptations of Satan, recorded earlier by Matthew. Satan had challenged the Savior to perform such extraordinary deeds as changing rocks to bread (Matthew 4:3) and hurling himself from the pinnacle of the temple (4:6). Jesus' enemies, taking up that blasphemous refrain, now challenge him to leave the cross. They are Satan's agents.

Fifth, the blasphemers once again repeat the charge—originally made in the house of the high priest (Matthew 26:61)—that Jesus would destroy the temple (27:40). It is likely that Matthew's first readers had already seen the temple's destruction by the Romans in AD 70 and would appreciate the irony of the accusation (cf. 21:41, 43).

Sixth, Matthew understands these mockeries as the fulfillment of biblical prophecy (Matthew 27:42–45). He does this by wording the taunts in language evocative of the Psalter:

> All those who see me ridicule me;
> They shoot out the lip, they shake the head: "He trusted
>   in the Lord, let Him rescue him;
> Let Him deliver him, since He delights in him!'"
> (Psalm 22:7–8)[5]

Thus, Jesus' enemies stand self-accused, becoming the very mockers in the psalm.

Matthew may also have had in mind the scorn of the mockers against the just man in the Wisdom of Solomon:

> Let us see then if his words be true, and let us prove what shall happen to him, and we shall know what his end will be. For if he be the true son of God, He will defend him, and will deliver him from the hands of his enemies. Let us examine him by outrages and tortures, that we may know his meekness and try his patience. Let us condemn him to a most shameful death. (Wisdom of Solomon 2:17–20)

ONE FINAL KINDNESS

Referring to the two thieves who died on either side of Jesus, Mark's account testifies, "Those who were crucified with him reviled him" (Mark 15:32).

At least they did so for a while. During the course of those three hours, however, one of the condemned thieves came to think better of the matter, as he watched Jesus hang there in patience, praying for his persecutors. Luke describes the scene:

> Then one of the criminals who were hanged blasphemed him, saying, "If you are the Messiah, save yourself and us." But the other, answering, rebuked him, saying, "Do you not even fear God, seeing you are under the same condemnation? And we indeed justly, for we receive the due reward of our deeds; but this man has done nothing wrong." Then he said to Jesus, "Lord, remember me when you come in your kingdom." And Jesus said to him, "Amen, I say to you, today you will be with me in Paradise." (Luke 23:39–43)

This scene with the repentant thief records the only "conversation" Jesus has on the cross. Since it is found only in the gospel of Luke, it is to this gospel that we should turn to understand it. We may divide our attention between the immediate context, which is the Crucifixion, and the wider context of Luke's gospel as a whole. Let us treat these in reverse order.

With regard to the larger literary context—Luke's gospel as a whole—two points are particularly noteworthy in this story of the thieves.

First, in drawing a contrast between the two thieves, Luke follows a pattern of antithesis that he employs throughout his entire narrative. For instance, it is Luke who immediately opposes the Beatitudes with the Woes (Luke 6:20–26). It is Luke who elaborates in detail the difference between the Pharisee and the woman who came into his house (7:44–47). It is Luke, likewise, who contrasts two men who went up to the temple to pray (18:9–14), the two sons of the same father (15:27–32), the rich man and the pauper (16:19–22), the faithful and unfaithful servants (12:35–40), the thankful leper and his nine companions (17:17–18), and the rich donors and the poor widow (21:1–4). Luke's opposition between the two thieves, then, is the climax in a lengthy series of contrasts.

Second, Luke's repentant thief is the final example of individuals who confess their guilt in the hope of obtaining divine mercy. Earlier instances include the publican in the temple (Luke 18:13), the Prodigal Son (15:21), and the repentant woman (7:36–50).

In all of these examples, Luke's narrative resonates with the Pauline emphasis on justification by faith. While in each of these examples the characters come to God with no justifying works of their own, this note is especially obvious in the thief on the cross who turns to Jesus for mercy with literally no time left to do anything except repent, plead, and die.

With respect to Luke's immediate context, the scene on Calvary, Jesus' conversation with the thief suggests three considerations.

First, this episode with the thieves is the second of three times that Jesus is pronounced innocent in Luke's account. The first pronouncement was made by Pilate and Herod (Luke 23:14–15), and the third will issue from the lips of the centurion under the cross (23:47). This verdict of the penitent thief, then, is added to the chorus of those who profess Jesus to be executed unjustly (23:41).

Second, the blasphemy by the unrepentant thief is the third and culminating instance in which the crucified Jesus is reviled in identical terms. First, there were the Jewish rulers who challenged Jesus to *save* himself if he was the Messiah (Luke 23:35). Then the

Gentile soldiers defied him to *save* himself, if he was a king (23:37). Finally, the unrepentant thief challenges Jesus to *save* himself, adding "and us" (23:39). We observe that the same verb, "save" or *sozein*, is used in all three instances. The thief's reviling of the Lord thus forms a climax to the theme of "save."

This sequence of blasphemy prepares for its foil—the scene's culminating irony—in which only one man, the "good thief," perceives the true path to being "saved." He boldly lays hold on the true meaning of Jesus' death: salvation! He is the "good thief," indeed; in this last, boldest, and most ironic act of theft, he leans over to one side, says a few words, and snatches hold of eternal life!

Third, in Luke's narrative the encounter with the two thieves immediately precedes Jesus' death so that his words to the second thief, promising to meet him that day in Paradise, are the last recorded words of the Savior to another human being during his earthly life. This final kindness, his message to the thief, represents the last thing Jesus has to say to his disciples on this earth.

Luke's gospel has now come full circle: When Jesus began his public ministry, his first sentence to the human race began with the word "Today" (Luke 4:21). On the cross, his final sentence to the human race begins with the word "Today."

TASTING DEATH

Evidently there were several "final words" of Jesus on the cross, some recorded in Matthew and Mark, others in Luke and John. As we have just observed, only Luke narrates the conversation with the thief. Luke alone, likewise, records the two times Jesus cries out to God as "Father": "Father forgive them for they know not what they do," and "Father, into your hands I commend my spirit" (Luke 23:34, 46).

John, an eyewitness to the Savior's death, tells how the dying

Jesus committed to him the future care of his mother (John 19:26–27).

As for Matthew and Mark, they both testify that "Jesus cried out again with a loud voice, and yielded up his spirit" (Matthew 27:50; cf. Mark 15:37), but neither author relates what the "loud voice" said. One conjectures that Matthew and Mark are alluding to Jesus' final words as they are recorded in Luke and/or John.

Let us begin, then, with the "second to last" sentence of Jesus, as transmitted by Matthew and Mark, who cite it in an Aramaic/ Hebrew mixture: "'*Eli, Eli, lama sabachthani?*' that is, 'My God, my God, why have You forsaken me?'" (Matthew 27:46; cf. Mark 15:34).

This anguished cry of the Savior has been variously interpreted. In particular, there has arisen, in recent times, the notion that God the Father actually *did* forsake His Son hanging on the cross. Jesus' abandonment by his Father—his experience of damnation—is sometimes understood, indeed, to be the very price of salvation.

This theory should be examined with a certain measure of caution, I believe. I suggest that the following points should be considered with respect to this caution.

First, the Christian faith firmly holds—as a doctrine not subject to contradiction—that the true God *never* abandons those who call upon him in faith.

Second, whatever Jesus' experience was—as expressed in this cry—it was still an *experience*. That is to say, it was existential; it pertained to Jesus' existence, not his being, or essence. In his being, or essence, Jesus remained God's eternal and beloved Son. Consequently, it was not possible that his cry of dereliction declared, as a *fact*, that God had abandoned him.

For those who, like me, follow the doctrinal guidance of Ephesus and Chalcedon, it was not possible for God the Father to forsake his Son in any *real*—factual—sense, because the Father and the Son are of "one being" (*homoousios*). The godhead is indivisible.

God does not abandon his friends and loyal servants—much less His Son.

Therefore, Jesus' cry conveyed not an objective, reified condition of his being, but rather his *human experience* of distance from God. The abandonment was psychological, not ontological.

It often happens that God's friends and loyal servants *feel* abandoned, and they feel it very keenly. And when they do, they often enough have recourse to the book of Psalms . . . as Jesus does in the present case.

When the Savior expressed this painful experience in prayer, the opening line of Psalm 22 arose to his lips—in Hebrew, *'Eli, 'Eli, lamah 'azavtani*—"My God, my God, why have You forsaken me?" He could hardly have prayed this line of the Psalter unless he knew the Father was still *"my God."*

In making this prayer his own, Jesus was hardly expressing a sentiment unique to himself. He was, rather, identifying himself with every human being who has ever felt alienated from God, abandoned by God, estranged from God. Jesus became, *for us,* what the ram in the thorns became for Isaac. That is to say, in making this very human prayer, Jesus expressed oneness with the rest of humanity so that (in the words of a Baptist friend of mine) "the full weight of the curse fell upon the Son as sin-bearer, the fulfillment of both the scapegoat, and the sacrifices of the old covenant. Jesus, thus, experienced every aspect of the curse: death, exile, broken communion with God."

Perhaps this prayer best expresses what we mean when we speak of "the days of his flesh" (Hebrews 5:7). It was in this deep sense of dereliction that we perceive, most truly, that "the Word became flesh and dwelt amongst us" (John 1:14).

After he prayed the first line of Psalm 22, did Jesus go on to finish that psalm silently? Christians have always suspected that this was the case. Continuing the psalm, he told the Father such things as this:

All the ends of the world
Shall remember and turn to the Lord,
And all the families of the nations
Shall worship before You.
For the kingdom is the Lord's,
And He rules over the nations. (Psalm 22:27–28)

I wonder, moreover, if we should stop with Psalm 22. Indeed, why would we? Let us imagine, rather, that Jesus, as he was dying, continued praying the next several psalms after Psalm 22. If he went on, quietly praying the subsequent psalms, Jesus' next words after Psalm 22 were: *Adonai ro'i, lo' 'ehsar*—"The Lord *is* my shepherd / I shall not want."

It is not difficult to think of Jesus going on with the other psalms in this sequence:

Lift up your heads, O you gates!
And be lifted up, you everlasting doors!
And the King of glory shall come in. . . .
Show me Your ways, O Lord
Teach me Your paths. . . .
The Lord is my light and my salvation
Whom shall I fear?
The Lord is the strength of my life
Of whom shall I be afraid? (Psalm 24:7; 25:4; 27:1)

If Jesus did pray this short sequence of psalms, it took only a few minutes for him to reach Psalm 31:5, which Luke identifies as his final words on the cross: "Into Your hands I commend my spirit" (Luke 23:46). Indeed, I suspect that these were the very words—recorded by Luke—to which Matthew and Mark refer when they tell us: "Jesus cried out again with a loud voice, and yielded up his spirit."

When we speak, even today, of *excruciating* pain, we do well to look at the etymology of that adjective: *ex cruce*, "out of the cross." It is nearly impossible to exaggerate what the Savior suffered on the cross.

Whether the cause of his death was asphyxiation or hypercarbia or hypovolemic shock or heart failure or exsanguination, or total physical exhaustion brought on by tetanic contractions throughout his entire body—or any combination of these, or any other plausible suggestion—the astounding fact is that Jesus, at the very end, "cried out again with *a loud voice.*" From a medical perspective, this is surprising.

Surely, it was the last thing anyone on Calvary could have expected. This "loud voice" demonstrated, nonetheless, the truth of the Savior's claim:

> I lay down my life that I may take it again. No one takes it from me, but I lay it down of myself. I have power to lay it down, and I have power to take it again. (John 10:17–18)

Jesus did not simply die. He willingly *tasted* death, according to the epistle to the Hebrews. He deliberately went through the actual experience of dying. The Gospels indicate that Jesus was conscious and self-aware to the end. There was no coma, no disorientation, no mental befuddlement. The Gospels testify, in fact, that he declined a narcotic that would have disguised and muted his pain.[6] The man Jesus *knew* what he was doing.

He knew, moreover, *why* he was doing it. It is remarkable that his disciples—then and now—express the conviction that Jesus, in the act of dying, thought of *them* and poured out his life for *each* of them. This is the testimony of the epistle to the Hebrews:

> But we see Jesus, who was made a little lower than the angels, for the suffering of death crowned with glory and honor, that he,

by the grace of God, might *taste death for every person*. (Hebrews 2:9, emphasis added)

Hebrews says, "for every person" (*hyper pantos*), not "for all persons" (*hyper panton*). Although Jesus certainly died "for everyone," it is important to remark that he died "for every *one*." In the mind and intent of Jesus, the beneficiaries of his death were not an amorphous group. The Good Shepherd, who gives his life for the sheep, "calls his own sheep *by name* and leads them out" (John 10:3, emphasis added).

More than two decades after the event, someone who had not known Jesus on earth was so confident on this point that he declared,

I have been crucified with Christ; it is no longer I who live, but Christ lives in me; and my life in the flesh I live now by faith of God's Son, who *loved me* and gave himself *for me*. (Galatians 2:20, emphasis added)

Such has been the conviction of believers down through the ages, those millions *in the flesh*, who have declared, unto their dying breath, "He loved me. He gave himself for me."

THE THREE THAT BEAR WITNESS

The description of the Savior's death in the gospel of John shows every sign of conveying the testimony of an eyewitness. Indeed, the Sacred Text itself calls attention to the firsthand reliability of this testimony: "And he who has seen has testified, and his testimony is true; and he knows that he is telling the truth, so that you may believe" (John 19:35). John alone includes the gentle detail "And bowing his head . . ." (19:30).

Two details in John's testimony seem worthy of special examination.

First, in its description of the moment Jesus died, John's very suggestive wording is unique among the four Evangelists: *paredoken to pnevma* (John 19:30). Generally, alas, that uniqueness is obscured in the standard English translations. They usually run something like this: "And bowing His head, He gave up His spirit" (NKJV). I confess that I have not found an English translation that differs substantially from this.

Such translations are seriously inadequate. *Paredoken to pnevma*, wrote John. To translate this as "He gave up His spirit" deprives the sentence of most of its meaning. Taken literally (which is surely the proper way to take him), John affirms, rather, that Jesus "handed over the Spirit."

That is to say, the very breath, *pnevma*, with which Jesus expired on the cross becomes for John the symbol and transmission of the Holy Spirit that he confers on the church gathered beneath his cross. Support for this interpretation is found in the risen Lord's action and words to the apostles in the Upper Room in John 20:22, "He *breathed on them*, and said to them, 'Receive the Holy Spirit [*Labete Pnevma Hagion*].'"

Consequently, John's description of the death of Jesus—"He handed over the Spirit"—portrays the Holy Spirit as being transmitted from the body of the Savior hanging in sacrifice on the altar of the cross. It is John's way of affirming that the mission of the Holy Spirit is intimately and inseparably connected with the event of the cross. The Spirit flows *from his flesh*.

This interpretation, besides being faithful to the literal sense of the verb (*paredoken*, "He handed over"), is consonant with John's theology as a whole. It was the cross and resurrection of Jesus—what John calls his glorification—that permitted the Holy Spirit to be poured out on the church. John said earlier, "The Holy Spirit was not yet given, because Jesus was not yet glorified" (John 7:39).

Second, John records another detail of the scene not mentioned by the other Evangelists: "But one of the soldiers pierced his side with a spear, and immediately blood and water came out" (19:34).

Taken together, then, John speaks of three things issuing forth from the Savior's immolated body: the Spirit, the water, and the blood. These things have to do with the gathering of the church at the foot of the cross because this is the place where Jesus' identity is truly known: "When you lift up the Son of Man, then you will know that I AM" (John 8:28).

These three components—the Spirit, the water, and the blood—appear also in the cover letter for John's gospel as the "three witnesses" of the Christian mystery: "And there are three that testify: the Spirit and the water and the blood; and these three are one" (1 John 5:8).

Speaking of the gathering of the church at the foot of the cross, Jesus had declared, "And I, when I am lifted up from the earth, will draw all people to myself." John went on to comment, "He said this to show by what kind of death he was going to die" (John 12:32–33).

It is the gathered church, then, that receives the witness of the Spirit, the water, and the blood at the foot of the cross, thereby knowing the Son of Man's identity as the "I AM" who spoke, of old, to Moses.

12

RISEN IN THE FLESH

When the author of the epistle to the Hebrews speaks of Jesus "in the days of his flesh" (5:7), he does not refer, strictly speaking, to the Incarnation. He refers, rather, to the eternal Word's voluntary subjection to *man's fallen state*; he means the time of Jesus' *earthly* life, which ended in his death. The "days of his flesh" do not include the life of the risen Christ.

Yet the risen Christ is still "in the flesh" in the sense that he exists—and will forever exist—in his body. He is not a mere spirit. Indeed, he can tell the disciples, "Behold my hands and my feet, that it is I myself. Handle me and see, for a spirit does not have flesh and bones as you see I have" (Luke 24:39).

Through the massive disruption of his descent into the realm of death and his resurrection from it, there persisted the personal identity of the one Christ. The body that rose is the same body that had died: "What is sown in corruption, is raised in incorruption. It is sown in dishonor, it is raised in glory. It is sown in weakness, it is raised in power" (1 Corinthians 15:42–43). The risen Jesus is, in short, the same Jesus.

In the course of forty days after his resurrection, Jesus not only was seen by his friends; he also conversed with them. He communicated with them in ordinary speech, very much as he had done all his life.

For this reason, it is appropriate that our reflections on the humanity of Jesus should include some consideration of that time during which "he also presented himself alive after his suffering by many infallible proofs" (Acts 1:3). Certain stories of the risen Jesus call out for examination in this respect.

POST-RESURRECTION STORIES

Although the resurrection of Christ was the most important event in history, there were no eyewitnesses to it, and, consequently, we have no description of it.

What we have, rather, are the testimonies of those who saw and heard him—and even touched him—in his risen state. These accounts, analyzed from a literary and theological perspective, appear to fall into two categories.

The first category may be called *kerygmatic and apologetic.* That is to say, some of the post-Resurrection stories seem to have come from the Christian apologetic witness to the world. This is why, in these stories, there is a great deal of emphasis on the reliability of eyewitness testimony, much as there might be in a courtroom. Christian preaching had a case to prove. These accounts stress the perceived physical reality of the Resurrection in documentable terms. This forensic testimony must be clear and unmistakable, emphasizing the identity of the risen Jesus beyond doubt.

Indeed, before any of the Gospels were composed, there was already an official list of qualified witnesses well-known among the early Christians:

I delivered unto you first of all that which I also received . . .
that he rose again according to the Scriptures, and that he was
seen by Cephas [Peter], and then by the twelve; after that he
was seen by more than five hundred brethren at once. . . . After
that he was seen by James, then by all the apostles. And last of
all he was seen by me. (1 Corinthians 15:3–8)

In this text one observes the heavy emphasis on apostolic
authority; in the main, the people listed in this text were official
spokesmen for the church. They were the established witnesses, to
the world, of the Lord's resurrection (cf. also Acts 1:21–22).

We find exactly this eyewitness emphasis in a couple of the gospel accounts.[1] This apologetic accent is rare and muted in the gospel
narratives, nonetheless. For example, the Lord's apparition to Peter,
although it is recorded,[2] is not described, nor do the Gospels mention a revelation to James, much less of a revelation to "more than
five hundred brethren at once."

There is a second kind of post-Resurrection story in the Gospels,
however, in which the literary and theological emphasis is very different. To appreciate this difference, we may begin by noting just who
is *absent* in that first type of story. What persons were *not* named in
Paul's list of the Resurrection's official witnesses? The women!

We should contrast this absence of the women in 1 Corinthians
15 with the prominence given to them in the Gospels themselves.
Here, these women disciples are the *first* to see the risen Lord, and
the apostles, whom Paul lists as the official witnesses, are described
as skeptical of the women's report![3] In the post-Resurrection gospel
stories, the apostles are *not* the witnesses; they are the ones *witnessed
to.* The *women* do the witnessing.

We read, for instance, "Now when Jesus was risen early the first
day of the week, he appeared *first* to Mary Magdalene" (Mark 16:9,
emphasis added), whereas in the official list in 1 Corinthians 15,

Mary Magdalene is not even mentioned. On the contrary, Paul says that the risen Jesus first "was seen by Cephas" (1 Corinthians 15:5). The contrast between 1 Corinthians 15 and the gospel accounts is striking in this respect.

This difference runs deep. In general the interest and concern of the four gospels is less apologetic and more theological and devotional. What we have in the Gospels are not quasi-forensic testimonies directed to the world, but the cherished memories of that first Paschal morning and the delirious ensuing days of the new spring.

Here we learn of Mary Magdalene's sentient recognition of Jesus' voice speaking her own name, the mysterious experience of the two disciples along the road and at the inn, and that early morning encounter at the lakeside, where Jesus served breakfast to the fishermen who had toiled all through the night. We behold the Lord's feet embraced by the women who lie prostrate in adoration before him. We see Thomas's trembling finger extended to touch the wounded hand of the Savior.

Now, we more clearly perceive in Jesus what I make bold to call his "light" side. There is something playful, almost teasing, in the way he meets and surprises his loved ones. The risen Jesus' manner has about it a glow of utter jocundity. *Christus Victor* is also *Christus Ludens*.

Jesus begins by asking questions that feign ignorance: "Woman, why are you weeping? Whom are you seeking?" "Children, have you any food?" "What kind of conversation is this that you have with one another as you walk and are sad?"

He resorts to a gentle and gracious irony: "Reach your finger here, and inspect my hands; and stretch out your hand, and place it into my side." "Do not cling to me; I have not yet ascended to my Father." "Bring some of the fish which you have just caught." "Come and eat breakfast."

Even the Resurrection angels take hold on the frolic of the day: "Why do you seek the living among the dead?" (Luke 24:5).

Let us inspect, then, some of these stories more closely.

MARY MAGDALENE

Little is known about Mary Magdalene, except that Jesus had delivered her from serious demonic influence (Mark 16:9; Luke 8:2). This liberation would explain why she referred to Jesus as "*my* Lord." We are also familiar with her loyalty to him, which drew her to the foot of the cross (Matthew 27:56; Mark 15:40; John 19:25). All the Evangelists, moreover, number her among the myrrh-bearers, those female disciples who received angelic testimony to the Resurrection on that glorious morning.[4]

In addition, the fourth gospel relates an apparition of Jesus to Mary Magdalene all by herself (John 20:11–18). Like the bride in the Song of Solomon (3:1–4), she rises early, "while it is still dark," and goes out seeking him whom her soul loves. In yet another image reminiscent of the Song of Solomon—as well as Genesis—she comes to the *garden* of Jesus' burial:

> Now the first day of the week Mary Magdalene went to the tomb early, while it was still dark, and saw that the stone had been taken away from the tomb. (John 20:1)

Lingering at the tomb in tears, Mary

> turned around and saw Jesus standing there, and did not know that it was Jesus. Jesus said to her, "Woman, whom are you seeking?" (vv. 14–15)

Here Jesus engages in what grammarians call the "erotema," the emotionally freighted question that sets a person up for a (usually pleasant) surprise. The question here playfully feigns ignorance on

Jesus' part. He fully intends to reveal himself to this brokenhearted woman, but he determines to do so in the course of a conversation in which she is engaged. Instead of getting a "news flash" about the Resurrection, she *discovers* it for herself in the sound of his voice.

Mary, however, who does not see very clearly through her tears, takes Jesus to be the gardener and answers his question in all seriousness: "Sir, if you have removed him, tell me where you have put him, and I will take him away." Then comes the dramatic moment of recognition, when Jesus simply pronounces the name by which he has always addressed her: "Mary!"

Mary Magdalene does not learn the Resurrection as an objective fact conveyed through the testimony of a third person; she grasps it, rather, in the sensitive recognition of the beloved voice that addresses her personally. Only at this point does she know him as *Rabbouni*, "my Teacher."

In this story, Christians are right to perceive in Mary Magdalene an image of themselves meeting their risen Lord and Good Shepherd: "the sheep hear his voice; and he calls his own sheep by name . . . for they know his voice" (John 10:3–4). This devout narrative of Mary Magdalene is an affirmation that Christian identity comes of recognizing the voice of Christ, who speaks the believer's name in the mystery of salvation: "the Son of God, who loved *me* and gave himself for *me*" (Galatians 2:20, emphasis added).

THE ROAD TO EMMAUS

For a few minutes the risen Jesus playfully concealed his identity from Mary Magdalene on Easter morning, but in the afternoon he carried this play much further, remaining unrecognized during a prolonged and detailed conversation with two other disciples:

Now behold, two of them were traveling that same day to a village called Emmaus, which was sixty stadia from Jerusalem. And they talked together of all these things which had happened. So it was, while they conversed and reasoned, that Jesus himself drew near and went with them. But their eyes were restrained, so that they did not recognize him. (Luke 24:13–16)

Jesus listens to their conversation for a while and then asks, "What kind of conversation is this that you have with one another as you walk and are sad?" This "ignorance" on his part persuades the pair that he must be "a stranger in Jerusalem," who has managed to miss the things everybody else has been talking about.

Jesus asks a second question, again feigning ignorance: "What things?" He listens while they inform him about his own death, their shattered hopes, and the very dubious report from the women who had been at the tomb that morning.

The reader is, of course, amused by the irony of this discourse. What I want to suggest here is that *Jesus* is amused by it as well. He strings these men along.[5] He will reveal himself to them in due course, but he first leads them through a process of learning:

Then he said to them, "O foolish ones, and slow of heart to believe in all that the prophets have spoken! Ought not the Messiah to have suffered these things and to enter into his glory?" And beginning at Moses and all the Prophets, he expounded to them in all the Scriptures the things concerning himself. (Luke 24:25–27)

The meaning of these Scriptures has been a preoccupation of Luke's gospel from the start. It was the burden of Jesus' first sermon at the synagogue in Nazareth. It was the subject of his conversation with Moses and Elijah on the mount of the Transfiguration. In the present scene, Jesus feigns ignorance precisely with a view to teaching these two disciples—and through them, all Christians to the end of time—his own understanding of the biblical text.

All of Christian doctrine is rooted, I believe, in Jesus' Paschal discourse to the two disciples on the way to Emmaus. The timing of that discourse is likewise significant, for it took place on the very day of his rising from the dead; on that day "the Lion of the tribe of Judah, the root of David," demonstrated that he "was worthy to take the scroll and to open its seals." He was worthy to do this because he was slain and had redeemed us to God by his blood (Revelation 5:5, 9). Jesus interprets Holy Scripture—indeed, he is the interpretation of Holy Scripture—because he "fulfills" Holy Scripture through the historical and theological events of his death and resurrection. His blood-redemption of the world is the formal principle of Christian biblical interpretation.

As for the two disciples on the way to Emmaus, Jesus continues to act his play to the end: "Then they drew near to the village where they were going, and he indicated that he would have gone farther" (Luke 24:28). This is at least the third time, since the trip started, that Jesus has teased these men in order to take the conversation in the direction he wants it to go. As though reluctantly—and only at their explicit invitation—"he went in to remain with them."

At last, Jesus' points of instruction having been made,

> he took bread, said the blessing, and broke it, and gave it to them. Then their eyes were opened and they knew him; and he vanished from their sight. (Luke 24:30–31)

The two disciples promptly turned around and headed back to Jerusalem. As they returned, they reflected that their hearts had burned within them as the Stranger had spoken to them on the way and had interpreted the Scriptures.

Luke does not say so, but one hopes they also apologized to Mary Magdalene and the other women for their unbelief.

A HARD CASE

Thomas was a pessimist. He belonged to that eminently practical school of philosophy, which can be summed up in two sentences, the first a hypothesis and the second an imperative: "If anything can go wrong, it will. Get used to it."

Holding such a view, a person can never be too cautious, or he risks getting too rosy a picture of things. Near every silver lining, after all, lurks a cloud. Classical philosophy was interested in the meaning of life. Not Thomas. He is more interested in getting through life without falling to pieces. He tightens the reins on enthusiasm and dissuades his heart from anything faintly resembling hope. The last thing Thomas would trust is a bit of good news.

Although he is known to history as "Doubting Thomas," I have always suspected that his doubting had less to do with his episte-mological system than with his nervous system. Ever brave to drain the draught of sadness and misfortune, he dared to imbibe joy, if ever, only in small sips. If there was one thing Thomas knew how to handle, it was bad news. This was his specialty.

It came as no great surprise to Thomas, then, when he learned that disaster lay just down the road. Indeed, Thomas was the first among the apostles to embrace the imperative of the cross. Unlike Peter ("Get behind Me, Satan!"), Thomas put up no resistance to the news. When Jesus declared his intention of going south to "wake up" Lazarus, the other apostles expressed their fear at the prospect. "Rabbi," they answered, "lately the Jews sought to stone you, and are you going there again?" It was Thomas who accepted the tragedy of the thing: "Let us also go, that we may die with him" (John 11:8, 16).

Thomas may also have been something of a loner, which would explain why, when the risen Lord paid his first visit to the assembled apostles, Thomas "was not with them when Jesus came" (20:24). One speculates that he may have gone off to get a better grip on himself. It had been a very tough week, after all. Just as Thomas had suspected it would, Jesus' life ended in tragedy. This, the apostle was sure, was the biggest tragedy he had ever seen.

Yet he was coping with it, somehow. Years of an inner docility to inevitable fate had schooled him in the discipline of endurance. Yes, he would get through this too. He was a man who could deal with misfortune and sorrow. Just don't disturb Thomas with hope.

He returned to the other apostles in the Upper Room that evening, having wrestled his soul into a quiet acquiescence. It was the first day of a new week. Thomas had faced down the disaster, and his control over his nerves was starting to return.

What Thomas had not anticipated, however, was that the other apostles, during his absence, would completely lose their minds. "Well, Thomas," one of them announced, "fine time to be gone. We have seen the Lord, and you just missed him!"

A whole week the risen Lord would make him wait, sharing that room with the ten other men to whom Thomas had hurled his challenge:

> Unless I see in his hands the print of the nails, and put my finger into the print of the nails, and put my hand into his side, I will not believe. (John 20:25).

As each day passed, the case for skepticism was strengthened.

But then it happened. The room was suddenly filled with a great light. New evidence had arrived and stood now undeniable on the scene. Thomas sensed that his long-established pessimism was about to be shaken. He rose and faced the entering light. He saw the familiar face and recognized the familiar voice: "Peace to you!"

We do not know if Thomas felt, at that moment, some urge to hide behind the other apostles. He was not given the chance. Turning to Thomas, the risen Jesus fully appreciated the irony of the hour. Nor would we be wrong, I think, to imagine a smile coming over the glorious face of the one who said to his beloved pessimist: "Reach your finger here, and inspect my hands; and reach your hand here, and place it into my side."

EPILOGUE—THE SAME JESUS

USING THE NARRATIVE THIRD-PERSON, THE EVANGELIST John describes his arrival with Peter at the tomb of Jesus:

> So they both ran together, and the other disciple outran Peter and came to the tomb first. And he, stooping down and looking in, saw the linen cloths lying; yet he did not go in. Then Simon Peter came, following him, and went into the tomb; and he saw the linen cloths lying, and the kerchief that had been around his head, not lying with the linen cloths, but folded together in a place by itself. (John 20:4–7)

Several questions about this kerchief thrust themselves forward: How was it that the two apostles observed and commented on this item? What does their observation tell us about the apostles? What did they conclude from the fact that the kerchief was *folded*? Finally, what should *we* surmise from that fact?

With respect to these questions, let us imagine the incident as part of a police report. Let us picture a detective asking the disciples to describe their discovery of the tomb, with all the details they can remember.

"Well, Officer," says John, "I arrived first at the tomb, but I did not enter. However, I did stoop down and noticed the linen burial cloths lying there. When Mr. Barjonah arrived, he went into the chamber ahead of me. He's the one that remarked on the kerchief. It was not lying with the linen burial cloths but was folded together in a separate place by itself."

"I see," says the officer, "the kerchief was folded. You are certain of this?"

"Yes," answers John, "the folded kerchief struck both of us as rather odd. Arriving at the tomb, we presumed that Jesus' body had been stolen. We did not credit the report of the women in our company who were all worked up, you see, talking about angels and resurrection and heaven knows what else. Their words seemed to us like idle tales, and we did not believe them. These sisters of ours had just experienced the trauma of Jesus' death late on Friday, so we thought them hysterical when they found the tomb empty.

"When Mr. Barjonah and I arrived there, our first impression of the scene suggested a grave robbery. That folded kerchief, however, was an inconsistent detail. Neither of us could imagine grave robbers stopping to fold that kerchief. This detail got us thinking."

Well, perhaps this detail should get *us* thinking too.

The kerchief, not lying with the linen cloths but folded together in a place by itself, was a point of firsthand eyewitness testimony. It puzzled Peter and John, challenging their supposition that the grave had been robbed. John recorded this item for the same reason he included so many other details of that week, namely: "And he who has seen has testified, and his testimony is true; and he knows that he is telling the truth."

Down through the centuries, no matter what conclusion a person might reach about Jesus' burial chamber, the folded kerchief has begged for an explanation: This detail gives the lie to any theory about grave robbery. Who folded it, and why?

We who accept the testimony of those first female witnesses know exactly who folded that burial kerchief. In the mind's eye we see him lying dead in the tomb, and then we picture his body responding to a new and completely victorious life. He stirs, he takes a breath, his heart begins to beat, his eyes open, as color and suppleness return to his flesh. Jesus is not resuscitated. He is risen. He has conquered death: "I am he who lives, and was dead, and behold, I am alive forevermore. Amen. And I have the keys of Hades and of Death" (Revelation 1:18).

That instant of the Resurrection was *the* decisive moment in the history of the world. It was the event of deepest importance for every human being who ever lived. It was the supreme *kairos*, the definitive "day of the Lord." The Law and the Prophets were fulfilled in that moment, and the existence of the human race took on a radically new meaning.

What, however, was the first thing Jesus did when the Resurrection life came surging into his body? How did he mark the moment in which the history of the human race stopped, suddenly, and went in a different direction? The simplest and plainest thing imaginable: he reached up, pulled the kerchief from his face, folded it, and set it aside, as though it had been a napkin used at breakfast. Those wounded hands, from which every grace would flow into the church until the end of the world, were first employed in a simple household task: folding a kerchief.

When Jesus folded that kerchief—his first action on rising from the dead—was the deed intentional?

Perhaps so. He may have done it very deliberately, for the purpose of leaving a tenacious clue for those who might inquire what happened in the tomb.

On the other hand, maybe not. The folding of the kerchief may have been completely unconscious. I do not find this hard to believe. The universal Christ, the eternal Word in whom all things subsist, was still the same Jesus to whom an act of elementary neatness came naturally. He may have done spontaneously what he did, much as someone else might unconsciously scratch his ear, or yet another look around for a stick to whack the weeds with as he walked along.

The risen Lord was the same particular person his friends had always known. He had just returned from the realm of hell, where he trampled down death by death. He was on the point of going forth as a giant to run his course. He was about to begin appearing to his disciples, providing them with many infallible proofs, being seen by them during forty days, and speaking of the things pertaining to the kingdom of God.

Nonetheless, he was still the same person, the same man, whose instinctive habits remained identical. He paused a moment to do what a deep, subconscious impulse told him should be done, what his mother had always taught him to do. He politely folded the kerchief and set it aside, and only then did the Lion of Judah stride forth to bend the direction of history and transform the lives of his fellow human beings.

APPENDIX—THE NEW ADAM

I APPEND THE FOLLOWING COMMENTS, LIFTED FROM THE writings of a major Christian leader and thinker of the fourth century, by way of suggesting the approach to the life of Jesus taken in this book is structured on parallels in ancient and traditional Christology.

As Christians meditated on the Pauline contrast between Adam and Christ (Romans 5; 1 Corinthians 15), they discovered further points of corresponding opposition between them. They perceived that each defect of man's fallen existence was matched by a specific remedy introduced into human experience by the life of Jesus, the incarnate Word. This came to pass, wrote Gregory Nazianzen, when "the new was substituted for the old." This happened, he went on, "because of philanthropy toward the one who had fallen through disobedience."

Gregory reveled in demonstrating how each of the various Christological "moments" recorded in the Gospels corresponded to some feature of Adam's fall: "each property of his, who was above all, was interchanged with each of ours."

Thus, the tree connected with the first sin was matched by

the tree on which Christ paid the price for sin, and "hands were set over against hands: in the one case, hands extended in self-indulgence, and, in the other, hands spread out in generosity; the first put forward without restraint, the second restrained by nails; hands driving Adam from the garden, and hands extended to the ends of the earth."

All of these things took place, wrote Gregory, for our training (*paidagogia*) and our healing (*iatreia*), "restoring the old Adam to the place from which he fell and leading him to the tree of life, from which the tree of knowledge had estranged him, because it was partaken of unreasonably and improperly."

Thus, too, the Virgin Mary, who introduced God's Word to the human race, takes the place of Eve, who introduced the human race to sin. Bethlehem supercedes Eden, and the manger replaces the ancient garden. Indeed, Gregory continued, "this is the reason the angels glorified first the heavenly, and then the earthly. For this cause the shepherds beheld the glory over the Lamb and the Shepherd. This is why the star led the Magi to adore and make offerings, in order that idolatry might be destroyed."

The healing of the ancient fall proceeded through the life and ministry of Jesus, the incarnate Word: "This is the reason Jesus was baptized and received testimony from on high, fasted and was tempted, and conquered him who had formerly been victorious. This is why devils were cast out, and diseases healed, and powerful preaching was entrusted to men of low degree, who proclaimed it fruitfully."

In all of these "moments" of the Incarnation, Christ was bringing remedy to Adam's fall: "This is what the Law, our schoolmaster (*paidagogos*), intends for us. This is what the Prophets intend, who are placed between the Law and Christ. This is what Christ intends, who fulfills the spiritual law. This is the reason for the emptied Godhead and the assumed flesh. This is the intention of the new union between God and man, one thing composed of two, and both existing in the one. This is the reason ... the economy, because of philanthropy toward the one who had fallen through disobedience, became a new mystery."

Gregory extends this comparison to consider the very nature of the Incarnation. He reasons: It is precisely because Christ is the replacement of Adam that Christ can be no less human than Adam—composed of both soul and body. As the whole human being fell in Adam, the whole human being was restored in Christ.

In the Incarnation,

> God was united to the flesh through the mediation of the soul, and such disparate natures were knit together by an affinity of each to the component that mediated between them, so that one became all for the sake of all, and for the sake of one—our forefather—the soul for the sake of the disobedient soul, and the flesh, because the flesh cooperated with the soul and was condemned with it. Christ, who was transcendent and beyond the reach of sin, did this for Adam, who had become subject to sin. (*Orations* 2.23–25)

The studied contrast of Adam and Christ, therefore, served another important function in the history of Christological dogma: although the councils of Ephesus and Chalcedon, in the fifth century, first gave dogmatic expression to these formulas of Christology—the unity of Christ in the duality of his natures— in the previous century we find the identical grammar and logic already in Gregory Nazianzen. For him, the complete humanity of Christ was an inference of his being the new Adam, the head of the human race.

NOTES

INTRODUCTION

1. Gregory Palamas, *Homilies* 4.12.
2. Cyril of Alexandria, *Letters* 46.
3. William Shakespeare, *Henry IV*, Part 1, Act 1, Scene 1.
4. All translations in this book (biblical and otherwise) are my own, though I confess to an informal and inconsistent "default position" in the New King James Bible.
5. Gregory of Nyssa, *De Opificio Hominis* 16.12; *Oratio Catechetica Magna* 6.
6. Irenaeus of Lyons, *Adversus Haereses* 4.20.7.
7. Gregory the Theologian, *Oration* 37.

1 GROWING UP

1. Cf. Acts 1:21–22; 10:36–37; 13:23–25. This historical point will be developed in detail in chapter 3.
2. There is nothing remarkable here. Genealogies in the Bible *always* follow the paternal line.

3. Flavius Josephus, *The Antiquities of the Jews* 16.2.4 § 43.

4. Cf. Luke 4:33, 44; 6:6; 13:10.

5. One hates to insist on the obvious, but the odor of Descartes and Schopenhauer still infects the cultural atmosphere.

2 TWO CONVERSATIONS

1. My translation here strives to convey the precise sense of the Greek expression in Luke 2:51; the imperfect tense *dieterei* means more than "kept." "Continued to keep" better expresses the ongoing action of the verb.

2. In the cultural setting of the day, marriage for a female at—or near—age twelve was not unusual.

3. Mark 1:14; cf. Matthew 4:12; Luke 4:14.

4. Mark 1:16–20; John 1:35–51; 2:2.

5. John 2:12; cf. Mark 1:21; Luke 4:23.

6. Matthew 2:1–15; Luke 1:8–38.

7. Mark 1:21–28; Luke 4:23.

8. John 16:32; cf. 4:21; 5:25; 13:1; 16:21; 17:1.

9. *Letters* 137 (to Volusianus), 3.9.

3 BAPTISM

1. Mark 1:7–8; John 1:29–34; 3:26–30; Acts 18:25–26; 19:3–4.

2. This emphasis is not added. It is conveyed in the Greek word order.

3. Contrast John 1:32.

4. Luke 5:16; 6:12; 9:18, 28; 10:21–23; 11:2; 22:32, 41–44; 23:46.

5. Prayer is obviously a major preoccupation of Luke. This gospel begins (1:10) and ends (24:53) with prayer. Luke is the only Evangelist to speak of Jesus at prayer also at the Transfiguration (9:28–29), in preparation for the calling of the Twelve (6:12), and just prior to the giving of the Lord's Prayer (11:1). Luke alone records certain parables about prayer (11:5–8; 18:1–14). Moreover, into her regular and standard formulations of worship, the Christian church

has, virtually from the beginning, adopted certain specific prayers found only in Luke: the Magnificat (1:46–55), the Benedictus (1:68–79), the Gloria in Excelsis (2:14), and the Nunc Dimittis (2:29–32).

6. Luke 1:15, 35, 41, 67; 2:25–27, 26, 27; 3:16.

7. The emphasis here is not added. It is contained in the Greek word order.

8. That is to say, his name was "Nathaniel, son of *Tholomew*."

9. Acts 8:14–15.

4 THE HUMAN CONDITION

1. I will not speculate on what sorts of divine "adjustments" were necessary for God's Son to become human. I know absolutely nothing about God's life except through the revelation of Jesus' life, given in Scripture.

2. We will come back to this Adamic motif when, in chapter 10, we reflect on Jesus' agony in the garden.

3. Cf. Zechariah 3:1–5.

4. Luke 9:51; cf. 13:22; 17:11; 18:31.

5. *Catechesis*, a word that literally means "according to the echo," refers to a standard pedagogical model in which the early Christians were instructed in the basics of the faith: repetition and memorization. Some of those "basics"—*archai*—are listed in Hebrews 6:1–2.

6. 1 Corinthians 10:1–13; Hebrews 3:7–4:11; 12:25.

5 THE PUBLIC MINISTRY

1. Luke 13:6–9.

2. Since as far back as the second century—Tatian's *Diatessaron*—there have been attempts to harmonize all the material in the Gospels into sequential narrative. Such efforts serve mainly, I believe, to distract the reader from the particular voice of each of the gospel writers. In liturgical practice, this harmonization approach is used exclusively during the Passion narratives of Holy Week.

3. It bears comparison with Luke's solemn introduction of the preaching of John the Baptist (Luke 3:1–6).

4. They even wondered, for a while, whether he was deranged; cf. Mark 3:21.

5. Outside of his seven "signs," John records a later miracle dependent on obedience to a command: "He said to them, 'Cast the net on the right side of the boat, and you will find.' So they cast, and now they were not able to draw it in because of the multitude of fish" (John 21:6).

6. The close relationship of Peter to "my son Mark" was well-known among the early Christians—1 Peter 5:13.

7. Matthew 8:1–4; Mark 1:40–45; Luke 5:12–16.

8. This was a liberty rarely taken by Jewish scribes copying Hebrew manuscripts. When a Jewish copyist found a biblical reading that looked wrong to him, or seemed unusual, he made a note of it, but he would not change it.

9. Matthew 9:18–26; Mark 5:21–43; Luke 8:40–56.

10. Their only shared feature, I think, is that the child is twelve years old and the woman has been bleeding for twelve years.

11. Matthew 8:23–34; Mark 4:35–5:20; Luke 8:22–39.

12. Papias of Hierapolis in Asia Minor, the Anti-Marcionite Prologue and the Muratorian Fragment in Rome, Tertullian in North Africa, Irenaeus of Lyons in southern Gaul, Clement at Alexandria in Egypt.

13. Nor do I discount the hypothesis that written sources were also available to the gospel writers. In particular, there seems to have been a written source from which Matthew and Luke derived a number of their parables.

14. Years ago, I sailed on the Sea of Galilee on a relatively calm day. There was only a slight wind, but the waves were high and the spray splashed up copiously over the sides. The scene as portrayed by Rembrandt catches the gospel account very well.

6 LEARNING AND TEACHING

1. I am leaving out of this discussion exactly what is meant by "the divine omniscience." If I were to deal with this subject, it would be necessary to mention that the concept of the divine omniscience is not quantitative. Divine omniscience does not mean that whereas we human beings know only *some* things, God knows *everything*. The difference between *some* and *every* is merely quantitative. Alas, this quantitative assessment does seem to be the fancy of those who think that the mind of Jesus was gifted with the divine omniscience. That is to say, they imagine that Jesus' knowledge extended, *quoad quantum*, to all things, as though divine omniscience were simply a widened extension of human knowledge. Even if a universal quantitative extension was a quality of the Incarnation—and there is not the slightest evidence for it in the Gospels—it would not imply that Jesus' mind was gifted with "divine omniscience." God's knowledge is formally—and not just materially— different from man's. Indeed, there are no parallels of comparison between the two. Between divine and human knowledge, there is no foundation for analogy or comparison.

2. Matthew 12:25; Mark 12:15; Luke 6:8; 11:17.

3. Perhaps this would be a good time to remind ourselves that we have not the foggiest idea what it means for God, as God, to be conscious of himself as God. It is insane to pretend we have the faintest inkling of what we are talking about when we speak this way. As Christians, who believe Jesus to be the sole mediator between God and man, we recognize that the only possible way for us to know how God thinks was for God's Son to assume a human mind—like ours—to think with. And that is what the Incarnation means with respect to Jesus' self-awareness. We must not kid ourselves here: Apart from Jesus, we have no insight whatever into the life of God. Apart from Jesus, all talk about God is just talk.

4. Matthew 8:26; 9:5; Luke 12:14; 17:17.

5. Matthew 12:5, 34; 19:4–5; 21:16; 22:20, 45; 23:33; Luke 11:40; 12:56–57.

6. Matthew seems deliberately to avoid this primitive usage, probably because of a reluctance to place Jesus within the same category as the Jewish leaders who opposed the gospel (cf. 23:7). In Matthew's story, Jesus is called "Rabbi" only twice—both times by Judas Iscariot (26:25, 49)! Indeed, it appears that, for Matthew, the title "Rabbi" was to be eschewed altogether (cf. 23:8). (With respect to the Semitic "Rabbi," it is worth remarking that not all Christians emulated Matthew's avoidance of the expression. In spite of the injunction to "call no man Rabbi," Christians in the Middle East, as late as the eighth century, felt no scruple about addressing their priest as "Rabbi" [cf. John of Damascus, *Letter on Confession* 9].)

7. John 1:49; 3:26; 4:31; 6:25; 9:2; 20:16.

8. John 8:4; 11:28; 13:13–14.

9. Mark 3:17, 22; 5:41; 7:11, 34; 10:46; 14:36; 15:34.

10. Mark 9:5; 10:51; 11:21; and, alas, 14:45.

11. Mark 5:35; 14:14.

12. Mark 4:38; 9:17, 38; 10:17, 20, 35; 12:14, 19, 32; 13:1.

13. Luke 7:40; 8:49; 9:38; 10:25; 11:45; 12:13; 18:18; 19:39; 20:21, 28, 39; 21:7; 22:11.

14. Matthew 8:19; 9:11; 12:38; 17:24; 19:16; 22:16, 24, 36; 26:18.

15. Matthew 24:45; cf. Luke 17:7–9; 22:27.

16. Matthew 9:28; Mark 8:27, 29; Luke 9:18–20.

17. Matthew 14:31; 16:8; 26:40; Luke 6:46; 8:25; John 14:9.

18. Matthew 10:29; 11:16; Luke 7:31; cf. 13:18, 20.

19. Other examples appear in Luke 11:11–12; 12:24–28; 13:2, 4; 16:11–12.

20. Matthew 17:25; 18:12; 21:28; Luke 10:26.

21. Mark 3:18; John 12:22.

22. This "road" (*hodos*) is, for Mark, the Way of the Cross. This word appears repeatedly as Mark's story carries Jesus toward Jerusalem to suffer and die (cf. Mark 8:27; 9:33–34; 10:17, 32, 46, 52).

7 JESUS AT PRAYER

1. Midweek services, which are standard in many Christian congregations, serve to express this truth about the structure of existence.
2. Mark 6:48; cf. Matthew 14:23–25.
3. Recall that only Luke mentioned Jesus praying at the time of his baptism.
4. Luke 9:51, 53; 13:22, 33.
5. 2 Peter 2; 3:3, 17.
6. 1 Peter 1:10; 2 Peter 3:2.
7. Matthew 10:2–4; Mark 3:16–19; Luke 6:14–16; Acts 1:13.
8. Matthew 11:25–26; 26:39, 42; Mark 14:36; Luke 22:42; 23:34, 46; John 11:41; 17:1, 5, 11, 21, 24, 25.

8 JESUS AND THE WOMEN

1. The Greek pronoun for "others" here is feminine.
2. Cf. Matthew 9:35–36; Mark 6:34.
3. Literally, "only begotten" (*monogenes*). Elsewhere, of course, this is the word used to speak of Jesus' own relationship to the Father (John 1:14, 18; 3:16, 18; 1 John 4:9).
4. Contrast this text with Matthew 9:18 and Mark 5:23.
5. Contrast this text with Matthew 17:15 and Mark 9:17.
6. Literally, "Stop weeping." In Greek, the present tense negative imperative (the form Luke uses here) means "Stop doing what you are doing." The common translation, "Do not weep," fails to catch this nuance.
7. Cf. Acts 10:36; 1 Corinthians 8:6; 12:3; Philippians 2:11.
8. Luke 10:1, 40; 11:39; 12:42; 13:15; 17:5, 6; 18:6; 19:8, 31, 34; 22:61; 24:3, 34.
9. It is used repeatedly in the post-Resurrection scenes.
10. Compare Mark 10:48.
11. Matthew 9:20–22; Mark 5:25–34; Luke 8:43–48.

12. The verb is in the Greek imperfect tense, signifying continued action.

13. The translation of *agathen* as "better"—instead of "good"—is required by the Koine Greek idiom, when two or more things are, in context, being compared.

9 THE GROWING CRISIS

1. We will presently reflect on this story at greater length.

2. Matthew 12:1–8; Luke 6:7–10; 13:14–16; John 5:9–10; 7:22–23; 9:14–16.

3. Matthew 12:8.

4. Matthew 9:1–6; Luke 7:48.

5. Matthew 21:12–17.

6. Matthew 21:1–9; Mark 11:1–10; Luke 19:28–40; John 12:12–19.

7. Thus, Mark indicates Sunday to Monday (Mark 11:11–12), Monday to Tuesday (11:19–20), Wednesday (14:1), and Thursday (14:12).

8. Matthew 9:1–8; Mark 2:1–12; Luke 5:17–26.

9. Matthew 9:9–13; Mark 2:13–17; Luke 5:27–32.

10. Matthew 21:33–46; Mark 12:1–12; Luke 20:9–19.

11. Mark 1:11; 9:7; Luke 3:22; 9:35.

12. Matthew 24–25; Mark 13; Luke 21:7–36.

13. 1 Kings 17:8–16; Luke 4:25–26.

14. Justin Martyr, *First Apology*, 67.

15. Matthew 26:26–29; Mark 14:22–25; Luke 22:17–20; 1 Corinthians 11:23–25.

16. Matthew 26:17–20; Mark 14:12–17; Luke 22:7–15.

17. Matthew 26:39, 42; Mark 14:36; Luke 22:42.

18. John 8:16, 18, 38, 49, 54; 10:25.

19. John 10:15, 17–18.

10 THE GARDEN

1. Matthew 26:36–46; Mark 14:32–42; Luke 22:39–46.

2. Origen, *Contra Celsum* 2.24.

3. John, who does not narrate the agony at all, goes immediately to Jesus' arrest, where the Savior is portrayed entirely in terms of dignity and majesty. In this gospel it is no exaggeration to say that Jesus *controls* the scene (cf. John 18:1–9).

4. Matthew 26:64; Mark 14:62.

5. John 18:36–37; 19:11.

6. Mark 5:37; Luke 8:51.

7. Matthew 17:1; Mark 9:2; Luke 9:28.

8. Matthew 26:40; Mark 14:37.

9. For reasons unnecessary to rehearse here, I am disposed to date Hebrews in the early 60s, prior to all four gospels. However, because none of the other accounts seems to borrow from Hebrews, the dating of these works is not pertinent to these reflections. Nor is the authorship of this work, on which Christians have never agreed.

10. To "taste death"—*t'am mitah*—was a standard rabbinical expression; see Matthew 16:28; John 8:52.

11. Matthew 26:39, 42; Mark 14:36; Luke 22:42.

12. Matthew 26:36; Mark 14:32.

13. Matthew 26:38; Mark 14:34.

14. Ambrose of Milan, *Commentary on Luke* (22:39–46).

15. Ambrose of Milan, *Homiliae in Lucam* 10.56.

16. Cf. Romans 8:15; Galatians 4:6.

17. Matthew 27:46; Mark 15:34; Psalm 22:1.

18. I am following the longer text of Luke, which contains 22:43–44. I am familiar with the weak manuscript support for these verses, but their content (the bloody sweat and the strengthening angel) is well attested in Christian sources either earlier than, or contemporary with, our oldest extant manuscripts of Luke. To wit, Justin Martyr, *Dialogue with Trypho* 103.8; Irenaeus of Lyons, *Against the Heresies* 3.22.2; Hippolytus of Rome, *Fragments of the Psalms* 1 (2.7); Epiphanius of Cyprus, *Ancoratus* 21:4–5.

19. Aristotle, *Historia Animalium* 3.19.

11   THE BRIDEGROOM IS TAKEN AWAY

1. Matthew 26:20, 26, 36, 37, 40, 58.
2. Matthew 26:31; Mark 14:27; 1 Corinthians 1:23.
3. Matthew 10:17; 20:19; 23:34; Mark 10:34; Luke 18:33; John 19:1.
4. For this reason, John reserves the name "antichrist" for those who deny Jesus' sonship from the Father (1 John 2:22; 4:2–3).
5. God's "delight" in His Son also evokes, once again, the opening chapter of Job.
6. Matthew 27:34; Mark 15:23.

12   RISEN IN THE FLESH

1. Luke 24:36–43; John 21:24–25.
2. Luke 24:34; cf. Mark 16:7.
3. Mark 16:9–11; Luke 24:11, 22–24.
4. Matthew 28:1; Mark 16:1; Luke 24:10; John 20:12.
5. Arguably, the closest biblical parallel to the present story is the account of Joseph, who "led on" his brothers for several chapters of Genesis, constantly feigning ignorance about their family, pretending not to speak their language, giving them various probative hoops to jump through, and at great length setting them up for the surprise of their lives, when at last he revealed to them, "I am Joseph, your brother."

INDEX

ABOUT THE AUTHOR

PATRICK HENRY REARDON IS PASTOR OF ALL SAINTS Antiochian Orthodox Church in Chicago, Illinois, and a senior editor of *Touchstone: A Journal of Mere Christianity*.

In the past forty years, Reardon has published more than five hundred articles, editorials, and reviews in popular and scholarly journals, including *Books and Culture* and *The Scottish Journal of Theology*. As a guest lecturer, he receives invitations year-round to give retreats, homilies, lectures, and Bible studies. In addition, Reardon has penned several books for Conciliar Press, including *Christ in the Psalms* and *The Trial of Job*.

Reardon was educated at Southern Baptist Theological Seminary in Louisville, Kentucky; St. Anselm's College in Rome; the Pontifical Biblical Institute in Rome; and St. Tikhon's Orthodox Seminary in South Canaan, Pennsylvania.